Still I Love

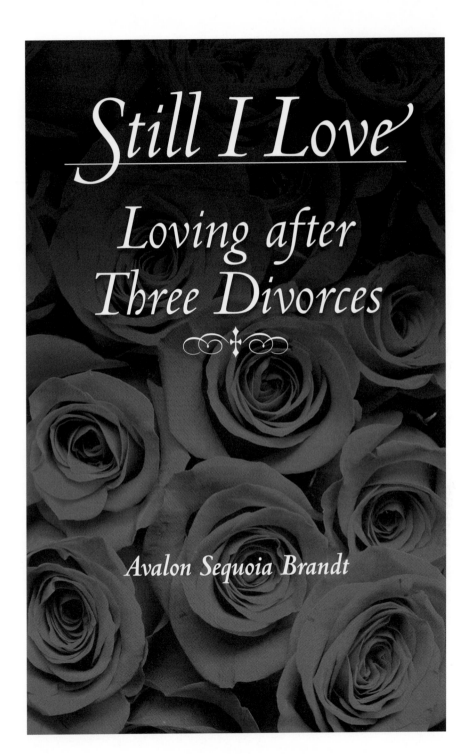

Still I Love

Loving after Three Divorces

Avalon Sequoia Brandt

ISBN-10: 0615981216
ISBN-13: 13-978-0615981215

Editor: Laurie Rosin, Sarasota, FL   www.thebookeditor.com
Copyediting: Sarah Novak
Cover and book design: Toelke Associates, Chatham, NY www.toelkeassociates.com
Printed by Versa Press, Inc., East Peoria, Illinois

This book is dedicated to everyone
In search of real love,
And to those who have found it
A sincere wish that you cherish your gift,
And to those who do not believe
In the power of LOVE
I pray that God will open your heart,
Set you free, and give you LOVE.

Contents

Foreword

This book is a must for those who want to better understand themselves and the forces that work against them. This is tough territory, but it is also real territory.

In this work, Avalon bares her soul and speaks of her own quest for understanding and meaning. Out of her own struggle she develops a theology of love and redemption that is worthy of further inspection. This work is a must for those who feel the tremors and quakes of the marriage built on the fault line.

Marriage is a marvelous institution that can be a tremendous blessing for two persons committed to their love. Many of us grew up watching the Hollywood marriages of Ozzie and Harriet, and June and Ward Cleaver. These marriages weathered every storm and found humor in the tensions and strife that hit the family. In later years we watched the Huxtables and saw the stability they had.

Much of our thinking about a good marriage was fashioned by these icons of marital bliss. In the midst of this public presentation, many persons saw the discontinuity between their experiences and the experiences of their television heroes. Our communities were not all built upon two-parent families, and many homes did not have simple-solution problems.

It is into this mix that Avalon comes with a fresh word about love and real marriages. Her abiding consult and comforter is God. Ultimately her love for God empowers her to find meaning.

For years Christians have tried to act as if our faith should ward off problems. The church has spoken eloquently of the standard but has left little assistance for those who have been forced for one reason or another to taste the bitter cup of divorce. It would be wonderful if all marriages could stay together, but it would be even more marvelous if the problems that broke the sacred cord had not existed or could have been managed. Not every Christian has been able to survive a marriage. Some, as the author points out, have had to struggle through tough decisions and tough realizations.

Read this work and let the grace of God provide you with the healing and encouragement that you seek.

Bishop Walter Scott Thomas, Sr.
Pastor of the New Psalmist Baptist Church

Introduction

I am not a psychologist; however, for the last twelve years while working as a civil litigator, I have listened to psychologists testify about the significance of nurturing children. They rarely use the word love to describe the facets of nurturing children and the consequences of not nurturing them. But regardless of the terminology, nurturing is synonymous with love and it should start at conception and continue consistently thereafter until we die.

What we all live for is to be loved and to love. Marriage is considered the epitomized expression of love and nobody gets married expecting to get divorced. I have been divorced three times — not because I wanted to but because circumstances forced me to make choices. None of my choices was easy and most of them were very painful.

My divorces left me brokenhearted but I am not bitter, angry, or regretful. After years of reflection and soul searching I find that still I love! I still love all three of my ex-husbands. You may think I'm crazy and you may ask why. I still love them because I understand that true love never dies.

Loving comes easy to me. It's natural and, although my dream for marriage has not been fulfilled, the constitution of my love goes far beyond marriage. My love is an eternal commitment rooted deep inside my heart and soul. I refuse to allow painful experiences and negative emotions to kill my love.

I will forever love and so should you! We all desire to be loved and true love is obtainable and sustainable for all of us who have a heart and are willing to embrace the reality that love can hurt.

My divorces gave me the opportunity to understand that the hurt that sometimes comes with love must be properly managed. Just as we deal with the other elements in our daily life, such as work, family, and money, we must all learn to manage our pain and disappointments from broken dreams and brokenheartedness in a way that always allows us to love.

I learned to manage my pain by controlling my thoughts, emotions, and actions. What we think determines how we feel, and how we feel dictates how we act. My emotions, and your emotions, sit at the base of our heart, and how we manage them is manifested in how we love. I learned that if I allowed fear, anger, regret, envy, hate, or doubt to overtake joy, determination, peace, laughter, perseverance, and a desire to be content, I would never experience love at the highest level.

My life is filled with people whom I love deeply. My life is also filled with people who love me deeply because love always multiples when it is applied. It is possible for everyone to have satisfying and fulfilling relationships. But in order to experience the fullness of true love, you must know how to control the negative thoughts, emotions, and reactions that come naturally from being disappointed, betrayed, and hurt.

After three devastating divorces, I could be angry. Some people have told me that I should be angry. I could have low self-esteem and be filled with regret. Instead I am secure, content, happy, and genuinely satisfied with my life. After all the years of tears and searching for answers, I still love!

It is my desire that everyone who reads this book will be filled with an understanding that love is available to us all! I hope you will be inspired to love yourself and others freely, unconditionally, and eternally.

Chapter I

Adam: My Childhood Sweetheart

My first husband was not named Adam. I chose the name to signify that he was my first love.

I grew up in a very loving family. My family is the basis for my ability to love so deeply. Since my birth, I have always been shown love by my parents, my sibling, my grandparents, cousins, aunts, and uncles.

When I met Adam I had already experienced the deep emotion of knowing that I was in love, because I was in love with my family and our lifestyles. But what I later discovered was that I could not duplicate all the characteristics of my family into my marriage and eventually I learned that I did not want to duplicate any relationship. I learned that every relationship is independent and what may be good for one relationship may not be good for another. It was a hard but valuable lesson!

I met Adam when I was about ten years old. We lived in the same neighborhood. We started as playmates, playing baseball in the alley and riding bikes. We would play together, all day, all summer long. I was somewhat of a tomboy. Even though I had dolls, I enjoyed playing a little rough sometimes.

Adam and I remained playmates until he became a teenager and no longer wanted to play with me — probably because he thought I was too young.

A few years passed and I didn't see Adam. Then it happened, it seems like only yesterday. I remember the events well. . . .

It was April 1975. I was almost fifteen years old. Adam had just celebrated his seventeenth birthday. I was completing the ninth grade and about to go to high school. Adam was already in high school.

On this particular day, my best girlfriend, Monica, and I were walking home from school. I noticed this cute guy driving by in this pretty white Monte Carlo.

I asked Monica, "Who is that?"

She replied, "You know who that is, it's Adam."

I didn't recognize Adam because what I saw, for the first time, was a mature, handsome young man. A hundred pleasant memories from our childhood playfulness filled my mind. I got excited.

Adam noticed us and stopped the car. I ran over to him, and we greeted each other with big smiles and pleasant hellos.

Adam asked me if I wanted a ride home, and of course I said, "Yes!" At first I forgot all about Monica. Adam knew her well and drove her home first.

I was captivated from the moment I jumped into the car. Adam lived one block from me. Monica lived only five minutes away, across the alley from my maternal grandmother, Mama.

Adam drove slowly and carefully. It was his mother's car.

We didn't do much talking during the ride. We listened to the music and sang. Adam and I both loved music.

When he dropped me off, he asked for my phone number. I was thrilled and quickly gave it to him. He called the next day, and thereafter we began to stay in contact. That day was a magical encounter.

I was intrigued by Adam's self-confidence. He was an A student in school. He played on the school football team, was a member of the wrestling team, and was an avid karate student. He had the respect of his peers.

Although he was aggressive in sports his demeanor was quiet and rather shy.

On June 10, 1975, Adam asked me to be his girlfriend. I was elated! I thought we were a young couple with great potential.

My parents began to trust Adam and allowed me to start spending more time with him. Adam would pick me up from school. My schoolmates knew him only as the cute guy with the pretty car. I loved it!

We began creating our own little world, spending endless hours on the telephone, closing out everyone.

Music was our passion. Every song that came on the radio was about love. It was through the music that Adam and I found love to be easy. We developed a strong bond, a bond that allowed us to live vicariously through the music. I dreamed of the day when we would be husband and wife.

My days were filled with anticipation of getting older, so that we could get married and fulfill my dream of being a wife and mother.

Adam became my best friend. I could talk to him about anything. We were honest and open, sincere and empathetic. We thrived on each other's ability to communicate. We laughed together and he shared my joy.

I am extremely extroverted and enjoy socializing. Adam is the opposite. So I gave up my socializing, to a point, and spent most of my time with Adam.

I was fascinated with the aura of Adam's protection of me. I always felt secure with him. I knew that he would protect me.

It seems that I poured myself into Adam and gave no thought to my own interests. There was only one thing that I wanted: I wanted to be in love and get married.

Adam was a great boyfriend. I could hardly wait for the day when he would ask me to marry him, when we would spend every day together as husband and wife.

My mind was flooded with a thousand images of how it would be. I wanted to give my heart and soul to this man. I wanted him to give me, in return, his heart, soul, and devotion.

We became inseparable. I believed that we were soul mates. We were young and yet very much in love.

Adam met all of my expectations for a boyfriend. He was intelligent and respectful and he was a gentleman. He opened the car door for me, just as I saw my father do for my mother and me.

Adam always made sure I was comfortable, asking if I wanted or needed anything.

Adam was romantic. We loved the low lights and soft slow music of the Isley Brothers.

Adam was responsible. He worked part-time at a restaurant. He used his money wisely, and he was never stingy. He took me out to dinner regularly.

Adam was also good looking. At seventeen he had a sensuous body, carved and molded like a sculptured athlete which only highlighted his shimmering bronze complexion. He was a stunning young man who was known by his peers to be a scholar and athlete.

Adam possessed all the qualities that I believed were necessary for a perfect match. My first love appeared to be a great catch. In my heart and mind I knew our relationship would grow to be deep and satisfying. I knew that we would be in love forever!

With time and a few years of maturing, our adolescent relationship had sprouted into a young adult love affair that everybody began to see.

In 1976 Adam graduated from high school and almost immediately enlisted in the U.S. Marine Corps. It was a surprising decision for everyone. Adam was already working and his family had expectations that he would further his education by attending Morehouse College in Atlanta. His aunt lived in Atlanta and she was prepared to make all the arrangements. I did not want him to go away, not to college and not into the corps.

At the time, I was in the tenth grade and my personal desire was to have Adam stay close to me. I pleaded and begged for him not to leave, but off he went to Parris Island, South Carolina, for boot camp. Adam's serious nature definitely prepared him for the most rigorous branch of the military.

I was deeply saddened by Adam's departure into the Marine Corps.

While serving in the corps, Adam continued on the road of eminence. While in boot camp he was appointed to the notable position of squad leader. Throughout his military career he received numerous meritorious promotions and excelled.

Adam was stationed far way from home. We would write to each other daily. Every day I would look forward to receiving my letters, in the pretty soft blue and white envelopes. Adam and I wrote about how we were coping being apart, how we missed each other, and how anxious we were to be together again. When Adam's four-year tour in the Marine Corps ended I had a few hundred love letters.

It was very difficult for me being so far apart. I remember one very impulsive moment when I called Okinawa, Japan, to speak with Adam. I had to talk with him because he wrote that he was seeing another woman.

I had no idea how to reach Adam in Okinawa. I started with the operator and asked her for information about locating Adam in Japan. After numerous directives from numerous operators, I was connected to Adam's barracks.

I was so happy when I finally heard his voice. It had been months since I had spoken to him. It was way too expensive. Nonetheless, on this one occasion I called halfway around the world to talk to Adam. I gave no thought to how much it would cost my parents, and it was one of the most expensive calls in my life. In 1977 a telephone call to Japan for just five short minutes cost over $60.00. Thank God I am Daddy's little girl. My daddy paid the bill, without much fuss, but my mother gave me a stern lecture about being responsible and spending money. At the time, talking to Adam was the only thing on my mind.

After our brief conversation Adam and I agreed to see other people, but vowed to love only each other. I trusted his love for me.

In early 1978, while Adam was stationed at Camp Pendelton in San Diego, he mailed me a box. The box was wrapped in brown paper and securely taped. Adam told me it was coming and he emphatically told me, "Do not open the box." When I asked him what was in the box, he replied, "Just don't open it." When the box arrived, of course I was curious. My mother asked me, "What's in the box?"

I replied, "I don't know. Adam told me not to open it."

My mother told Adam's mother about the box. Adam's mother asked me, "What's in the box?" I replied again, "I don't know, Adam told me not to open it."

I placed the box under my bed. For a few weeks, I didn't open the box, but of course one day my curiosity got the best of me. I got the box from under my bed.

I was careful not to tear off the paper because Adam had wrapped and taped the box like it contained the gold from Fort Knox. I opened the box and what I found inside shocked me. Inside was a gun.

I had seen a gun on only one other occasion, in the glove compartment of my father's car. This was the first time I touched a gun. There were no bullets in the gun and no bullets in the box. My curiosity satisfied, I placed the gun back in the box, sealed it with tape and put it back under my bed. I never told anyone.

When I spoke with Adam I let him know that I had opened the box, and he said, "I knew you could not wait."

I asked him, "What do you need with a gun?"

He replied, "I just got it, it was a good deal."

We went on with our conversation and I never gave the gun a second thought. If only I had known!

While Adam was away in the corps I continued my education. He was a positive role model for me and encouraged me to do well in school. He would not allow my dream for love to cloud my judgment on education. At sixteen I graduated from high school with an A average. I was shocked because although I knew I wasn't stupid, I had never given my education much thought. I knew I wanted to have a good job, but what I desired most was to have a husband and children.

While waiting for marriage I searched for a career. At one point I considered being a teacher, but after my mother got me a catalog from Coppin State College, and I reviewed the curriculum, I dismissed that career. Not until one of my high school teachers talked to me about a program for paralegal studies did I make my choice.

It was only a two-year program and it was in the legal profession, in which I had developed an interest. The program fit perfectly into my matrimony dream. I wanted to get married and start my family as soon as possible. I enrolled in the Community College of Baltimore City in the paralegal program.

In early 1979, while Adam was stationed at Camp Lejeune in North

Carolina, he surprised me.

My family had traveled to North Carolina for one of our routine visits. Adam agreed to meet us in Henderson and I anxiously awaited his arrival. When he arrived we greeted each other with a tight hug, big smiles, and a short kiss.

Adam checked into his hotel room and I went with him. We began talking about our upcoming weekend with my family and Adam reached in his pocket and pulled out a little black jewelry box. Adam placed the box in my hand and as I slowly opened the box, in a soft yet strong voice, Adam asked me to be his wife. I told him yes, put on the ring and ran out of the room to go see my parents. I was ecstatic but the excitement didn't last long.

My father asked me, without cracking a smile, what does the ring mean? I thought it was obvious, and my mother quickly interjected, "Let me see the ring." It was clear to me that my father was not excited that his little girl was going to get married, but it didn't take long before he grew to accept the fact.

In many ways Adam and I were still children, but we thought we were ready to take on the responsibilities of adults. I thought surely I was ready to set up house and be a wife, although I didn't know how to cook and I had never managed a bank account.

Adam and I selected a wedding date and the planning began.

In June 1979 I graduated from my two-year college with an Associate in Arts degree and a certificate in Paralegal Studies, but my graduation was not the highlight of that year. On Saturday, October 13, Adam and I were married. It was a beautiful day and everything that I had dreamed. I had eight bridesmaids, a stunning long white gown, a beautiful veil, and friends and family surrounding us. I was nervous but more excited than anything. Standing at the altar with Adam, I began singing Natalie Cole's

"Inseparable," for indeed Adam and I were inseparable.

Finally, Adam and I were husband and wife and we could start our life together.

Adam still had a month left in the Marine Corps. I was working as a legal secretary for a law firm located in Baltimore's newly constructed Inner Harbor. I thought it was a good start.

After coming home from the Marine Corps, Adam got a job as an electrician with a prominent electrical contractor. We were on the right track.

We rented an apartment and quickly furnished it and filled it with the beautiful wedding gifts.

I didn't know how to cook much of anything, but I could prepare Adam's three favorite meals: cheeseburgers, peanut butter and jelly sandwiches, and Kellogg's Frosted Flakes. Adam loved his mother's cooking, so we spent lots of evenings at her house for dinner. While I tried to learn to cook, we also ate regularly at my Mama's house.

Mama was my maternal grandmother. She stood about five feet three inches, weighed about two hundred pounds, and had a beautiful brown complexion. She was a solid woman, both in stature and size. She always wore lipstick with her nails painted perfectly. Mama was a wise woman and I always listened to her. She was the person who showed me how to love.

Our first year of marriage was good. All the troubles started right after our first wedding anniversary. Something was wrong. I noticed a change in Adam. In a short time something happened to us. I didn't know what it was. Our marriage started to go downhill too quickly for me to comprehend.

It was 1981 and the year started with problems between Adam and me. Usually when Adam got off work, he would come home, do some exercise, and wait for me to get off work. We had a routine. We had only one car, so Adam would pick me up at the bus stop and we would go home for dinner or to his mother's house for dinner. We had always made plans to do things together, but this year Adam developed a new routine. He got off work, picked me up from the bus stop, dropped me off at home, and went out. He would say, "I'm going out, will be back soon." He would tell me he was going to see his buddy, and I believed him. I would wait patiently for him to come home.

As time went on, I became frustrated and it became troubling to me. I didn't know what was happening. It seemed that almost overnight our marriage began to take a different path. Adam was out without me and I had no way of getting in touch with him — there were no cell phones in 1981 — and I desperately wanted us to be together.

When Adam would return home, sometimes very late at night, I would tell him that his actions were wrong and inconsiderate. He would say something that soothed my concerns, but it kept happening and I felt hurt and confused.

Adam and I decided we would move closer to our families. I also thought this would bring us back to our days of sharing evenings together.

At the end of our lease, we moved back to our childhood neighborhood. Adam started staying out even later at night. I began to suspect that Adam was fooling around. I wonder how adultery got the term "fooling around"? Do you think it could be because only a fool would commit adultery?

One night, sitting on the side of the bed, I boldly asked Adam, "Have you slept with anyone else since we've been married?" In my gut I knew what the answer would be, but nothing could have prepared me to deal with the blow of Adam's response.

"Yes I have."

We openly talked about his adultery. I learned that it wasn't just once. My heart flooded with pain. My life was falling apart.

I picked up a lamp and threw it on the floor. It shattered. I asked Adam and myself, "How did we get to this place?" Everything appeared to be good. We had a big wedding, beautiful wedding gifts, family, friends, laughter, joy, and lots of love. So what happened? I wondered, and I asked God, but there was never an answer. I doubt that any answer would have been satisfactory or acceptable because I didn't understand what was happening.

Despite how terribly crushed I felt, I had no intention of leaving Adam.

We talked about the problem over and over. I prayed about it and expected the trouble to go away and for everything to work out fine. At times Adam and I would pray together, but most often Adam would only listen to me pray.

He knew that I was a church girl, a young Christian. I was baptized at twelve and I attended my church every Sunday. I believed in God and the power of prayer. Adam had heard me over the years talk how much I loved the Lord. Adam was not a churchgoing man. He took me to church, just like my father took my mother, brother, and me to church. I was not concerned that Adam did not go to church, because my father did not attend church regularly, and I knew that he was a Christian. I believed that one day Adam would see the need to invite God into his life.

Now I was waiting for God to turn Adam around.

I continued to love Adam and hoped and prayed that things would turn around for us but, no matter how much talking, hoping, praying, and believing I did, Adam's late nights became more frequent. I thought I was losing my mind. What could I do? I couldn't run home to my parents. I was married and wanted to be with Adam.

I knew I had to fight for my marriage, but the pain was becoming unbearable. I stayed up all night, anxiously listening for Adam. I ran to the window expecting to see him walking up the path. I watched the clock, crying, as time ticked into what seemed like eternity. Hell had claimed occupancy in my home.

I didn't eat. I couldn't eat, because there was so much confusion in my mind. I kept trying to figure it out. I only knew I was not going to give up. I had to find the strength to fight to keep my marriage. I had to be strong, even though I didn't feel strong. I had to get courage, but courage to do what?

A girl began calling our house, asking to speak with Adam. When I asked what the call was about, she would reply, "I need to speak with him." I was only twenty and very timid. I tried to be polite and told her, "Please do not call my house or my husband." She ignored what I said.

I confronted Adam and he told me her name was Rhonda. He met her while roller skating. She was eighteen and in the twelfth grade.

I tried to be strong. I didn't tell my parents what was going on, but I confided in my best friend, Monica. She wanted us to follow Adam and confront Rhonda. I didn't want to because I was afraid of how Adam would react.

After over a month of Adam's coming home at two o'clock in the morning, I finally got the courage and strength to tell him I couldn't live that way anymore. If he couldn't come home at a decent hour and do the right things, I did not want him to come home at all.

Without fully understanding what I was saying, and what could be the consequences, I waited for Adam to say, "You are right," but instead he said, "I am going to get a place of my own."

I was left in despair. I thought I was relieving the pressure of being angry, only to trade anger for sorrow, depression, and confusion.

Despite what Adam was doing and not doing, I still loved him emphatically. I never doubted that he would one day be considerate to me and love only me.

Because of my strong belief in our love I never considered divorce.

Adam kept seeing Rhonda, and he took no steps to pack and move out.

It was February 1981, about six weeks after I learned of Adam's affair. I was worn out. I wanted my husband's devotion, yet I also wanted him out of my life. I'd already had enough.

One evening while he was out with Rhonda, I packed. I began the first awful stage of tearing down our marriage. I separated the wedding gifts, the towels, the dishes, the sheets, the pots and the pans.

I knew Adam wasn't leaving without all his stereo equipment and music. Slowly I began dismantling our home.

I was in so much pain and confusion that I cannot even adequately describe how I felt. I was too afraid and too embarrassed to tell my family. Divorce was frowned on by my parents and family.

When Adam returned home he was surprised to see his belongings at the door. He did not raise his voice or argue with me, he just got his things and left. It was Valentine's Day.

Adam moved into his apartment.

I tried to go on with my life, but it wasn't simple.

I was working as a paralegal and I prepared a legal separation agreement for us to sign. I didn't know what else to do.

Although we were separated Adam continued to call me and check on me. We also continued seeing each other. I started spending nights at his apartment and he started spending nights at what was now my apartment. It wasn't long before we reconciled and Adam stopped seeing Rhonda.

But then things began, at an alarming pace, to spiral downhill.

Rhonda was adamant about having Adam in her life. She persistently called Adam, like a stalker. She would cry, saying that she had been in a fight with her mother, that her mother was putting her out on the street.

Adam would run to her rescue. On one occasion I told Adam I wanted to go with him. I wanted to see what Rhonda looked like. I wanted to know why Adam couldn't stop seeing her.

We went to meet Rhonda. We pulled up to the corner and there stood Rhonda. She was a thin attractive girl.

She got into our car. We drove around the corner. Adam introduced us. I listened to her crying, talking about how her mother was putting her out of the house because she was seeing Adam. It seemed logical to me that if she stopped trying to see Adam, her mother wouldn't put her out.

After about thirty minutes of listening to Rhonda we dropped her off, on the very same corner where we had picked her up. She got out of the car, said good-bye, and went back home to her mother.

On the ride home, I kept thinking, this is unbelievable. What am I doing?

Why did Adam allow this to happen?

Again, I told Adam I was not going to tolerate him seeing Rhonda. It was the making of a fatal attraction.

Rhonda kept calling Adam. I begged her to leave us alone and she told me she would. But she never did. She would call and start crying, with the same story, that she had been in a fight with her mother and her mother was going to put her out.

I felt sorry for her. I listened to her describe the acrimonious relationship she had with her mother. I had always learned that Christ loves everybody.

I didn't love her but I couldn't hate her. I didn't know how I should feel.

After a few weeks of reconciliation, Adam and I separated again because he continued to see Rhonda. And just like before, we started seeing other each again. It started to feel like I was on a merry-go-round, not knowing which way to turn.

I felt myself dying inside, little by little, every day, but as badly as I hurt inside, I wouldn't let it show on the outside. Nobody suspected that Adam and I were having problems. Thank God I had Monica, who walked this painful path with me. She held my hand, listened as I cried, and, if it was time to fight, she was with me. Nevertheless it still hurt, real bad.

After a brief second separation, Adam and I reconciled again. We could not stay away from each other. I still had hope that we could repair our marriage. But our marriage had become a seesaw. We would separate and move clothes and stereo equipment from one apartment to another. Then we would reconcile and move the clothes and stereo equipment back.

I thought it must be love.

But nothing changed. Rhonda kept calling and Adam kept seeing her.

Adam and I separated a third time. This separation also lasted for a short period of time.

In May 1981 Adam and I reconciled again. I did it because I still loved him. I was not ready to give up on our marriage. I was not ready to face the public humiliation.

This time Adam attempted to implement our old routine, coming home from work, dinner together, music and laughter. He would tell me how happy he was to be home, that he loved me and that he was sorry for all the pain he caused us.

Inevitably the phone would ring and Rhonda would have some horror story. I must have changed our telephone number at least three times in six months but Rhonda always got the number, undoubtedly from Adam!

Adam would leave to help Rhonda, and then come back home to me.

This reconciliation was different. It was the beginning of the end.

Adam lost his electrician job. I learned that he had been missing days and weeks from work to be with Rhonda.

Adam could not make his car payments, and I didn't earn enough money to support our household. We were now struggling not only emotionally but also financially.

I finally told my family about our problems. They were very supportive. My parents paid our rent for a month and my grandmother gave us food.

Adam's car was eventually repossessed. I thought with Adam not having his car, we would go back to the times when we shared one car, when we spent our time together running errands and enjoying each other.

Instead of staying home and waiting for me to get off work, Adam rode his ten-speed bicycle to see Rhonda.

Adam didn't realize that things were getting worse for him, emotionally. I noticed that his complexion began to change, he became more introverted, and our communication dwindled to almost nothing. I knew he was about to lose his mind.

I tried to maintain my own emotional welfare. I kept asking God to help us.

In early June Rhonda announced that she was pregnant!

Rhonda's mother learned that Adam was married. She called me one evening and told me she wanted Adam to stay away from Rhonda. I thought, finally, it's over! I was wrong.

Something was different. Adam was now at home when I came home from work, but I felt inside that he was losing it. I would take off work to stay at home with him, and to prevent him from seeing Rhonda.

One Tuesday morning I was preparing to leave for work. I was now in jeopardy of losing my job so I had to carefully pick and chose the days I would miss.

This particular morning I wanted to stay home. Something was different. It was an eerie feeling. I knew something was happening!

I wanted to stay home with Adam, but I couldn't lose my job, too.

Our broken marriage, Rhonda and her pregnancy, his unemployment, our mounting bills — it was too much for him to handle. He lay in the bed looking at me, and I pleaded with him to talk with a professional. I was desperate to get him help because, in addition to all the problems we were already having, Adam was now sleeping with the gun under his pillow.

I was never afraid of Adam. I never feared that he would hurt me. I knew that he would die to save me. I was gravely afraid for him.

I tried to convince him to go to the veterans' hospital to talk with a psychiatrist. I told him that I would go with him, but he refused to go and reluctantly I left for work.

Immediately on arriving at work I began calling home to check on Adam.

I knew it was going to take time to get back on track, but I also felt that we were running out of time.

He and I talked several times during the morning. During our last conversation I knew something bad was going to happen. Suddenly, the operator interrupted with the announcement that she had an emergency call.

I knew it was Rhonda.

My heart stopped as the operator said, "I have an emergency call from Curtis. Will you hang up for her?" Curtis was Adam's best friend and I knew it wasn't Curtis because the operator said, "Will you hang up for her?" It was Rhonda. Before I could say no, Adam said yes.

After Adam hung up with me, I began trying to call him back. I called all afternoon. At first there was a busy signal, then, almost instantly, the phone began to ring.

Adam never answered.

I called my grandmother. Even though I had not told her what was going on with Rhonda, Mama was always able to soothe my fears, to say something wise that gave me peace and courage to go on. Coincidentally, without me even telling her what was going on, she told me that she had just spoken with Adam.

Mama told me that she told him to go to the hospital, that she was worried about him. She said Adam told her okay and he had to go. Mama and I agreed that Adam needed to get help right away, or else something bad was going to happen. Mama was a spiritual woman!

When five p.m. arrived I dashed from my job. On my way home I passed the gas station where Curtis worked. It had only been a few days since Adam had regained possession of his car. It had been repossessed and my aunt had helped us get it back. I was surprised when I saw the car parked at the gas station because I did not see Adam or Curtis. This seemed strange to me but I did not stop because my intuition told me to go home. I just kept driving.

I arrived home, back into the painfulness of knowing Adam was out with Rhonda. I thought, here we go again, but this evening was particularly overwhelming. I was hysterical with the anxiety, the anticipation of when Adam would come home. I thought I was losing my mind.

The time passed slowly, six o'clock . . . seven o'clock. . . . I knew the pattern and, by eight o'clock, I was in a rage.

I called my mother screaming and crying for my father to come right over. Instead, my mother sent my Uncle Joe and Monica's mother. They were only five minutes away and my parents lived twenty-five miles away.

Uncle Joe and Monica's mother, Samantha, arrived at my apartment. I was hysterical, crying, screaming, running from room to room, banging on the walls, stomping my feet.

My meltdown had come! Samantha gave me a sleeping pill. I eventually went to sleep.

Around three a.m. I was awakened by the telephone. It was Adam.

Adam said, without stumbling over his words, "Somebody killed Rhonda's mother." I began to tremble. I asked Adam if he was certain she was dead, and he replied, "Very."

Questions flooded my mind. When? Where? How?

Adam said, "It was a burglar. She was shot five times."

I asked, "Where is Rhonda?" Sympathy began to fill my heart.

"She is right here. We are at the hospital."

With sincere compassion and empathy, I told Adam to tell Rhonda that I was sorry about her mother's death.

He said, "Okay, I'll call you later."

Placing the receiver in the cradle, I thought, Oh, my God, they killed her! I just knew they killed her.

The next day I didn't see or hear from Adam.

I asked my father to come over and change the locks on my apartment door. I was afraid for my life, although I tried to convince myself that I shouldn't be afraid. I also asked Daddy to take all of Adam's clothes to his mother's house so Adam would not have an excuse to come to the apartment.

Several days went by before two detectives, one female and one male, came to my apartment to ask me questions. When is your husband's birthday? Does he have a gun? Do you know Rhonda?

I told them that I would not answer any questions, and I wanted them to leave. I did not want to answer any questions because anything I said could have been misconstrued and used against me or Adam. Regardless of my refusal to answer any questions, they continued to ask them. Finally I called my boss, an attorney, and asked him to tell the detectives to leave me alone. He was well aware of the trauma in my marriage and had been very supportive. I shared my problems with him when I was reprimanded for taking too much time off. He desperately wanted me to get my life together and leave Adam.

After speaking to my boss, the detectives left with no information from me. I locked my apartment door and breathed a sigh of relief.

I was living a nightmare.

A few days passed and still I had not heard from Adam. It was the end of June. The warm and rainy night was jolted by spectacular lightning and crashing thunder, the winds cast their horrific tremors, when suddenly the sky lit up like a flashlight and then the electricity in my neighborhood went out. It was pitch-black dark. The thunder continued erupting like bombs set off to destroy the earth.

Unexpectedly, there was a knock at my door. Who could it be? I crept to the door. "Who is it?"

It was Adam.

Something inside me said, do not open the door. I asked, "What do you want?"

He whispered softly, "I need to talk to you and I want to get some of my clothes."

I was afraid. I stood there in the dark, listening to the rain, watching the lightning, dreading the loud hard sound of the thunder. I kept the door locked. My only thoughts were to tell Adam I had nothing to say, that his clothes were now at his mother's house, and I had no intention of opening the door.

The fear inside me grew. Finally, Adam left.

Just as fast as the thunderstorm started, it ended. Minutes after Adam left, the lights came on.

I was startled when the phone rang. It was Adam. He had gone to his mother's house and called to apologize. I knew that he wanted to talk with me. I knew he wanted me to help him, but I could not talk or listen to him. I was too afraid to trust him.

I faced one of the most difficult decisions in my life. Should I stand by him or protect myself?

I asked him, "Where is Rhonda?"

He replied, "In the car."

My mind began to race. Had he come to my apartment to kill me? Rhonda's mother was out of the way. Now Rhonda wanted me out of the way.

Maybe if Rhonda had not been with Adam, I would have talked with him, but I could not go where I knew danger was waiting for me.

I had no idea how I was going to make it through this nightmare. I do not know how I made it day to day, except God kept me going when I couldn't keep myself going.

I couldn't tell my family everything. I couldn't tell Adam's mother everything. I carried the awful secret that I thought Adam and Rhonda had plotted to kill her mother. I told Monica my suspicion and she kept saying, "I don't believe this is happening." We were both in shock!

Hell was quickly attempting to pull me into its pit and kill me.

It was a beautiful July day but there was no sunshine in my life. Adam called me the afternoon of Rhonda's mother's funeral. He said that he had attended the funeral with Rhonda and sat on the back row. He sounded like he was in agony. I couldn't imagine how he was functioning.

I tried to cope and act as if nothing was wrong, but everything was wrong. Later that day Monica and I were headed to Adam's mother's house for a cookout. As I drove down the street, Monica and I noticed Adam's car coming toward us. Rhonda was driving. I thought that was so strange because her mother's funeral had been only a few hours earlier. I expected her to be distraught and fatigued. She didn't appear to be sad or worried.

As the cars passed, I noticed Adam in the passenger seat looking like a limp and lifeless child. I would have thought that it was his mother's funeral, the way he looked. It was spooky!

It seemed as though we traveled in slow motion and a bad movie was playing before my eyes.

Monica and I arrived at my mother-in-law's house. I felt sick inside. Why did I have to see them? I parked my car, and Monica and I went inside. Adam's mother immediately told us that Adam and Rhonda had just left.

I was hurt to learn that Adam felt comfortable enough to bring Rhonda to his mother's house. When Adam first starting seeing Rhonda I asked my mother-in-law to talk to him about his infidelity, but she refused. She said that she did not want to get involved and I accepted her decision. I was so glad we weren't all together inside the house. I could only imagine how bad it would have been for me.

I did not want to be continually reminded of the horrible facts of my life. I felt like I wanted to die.

Every day I tried to go on like everything was fine. Only one thing was on my mind. They did it. They killed her mother!

At two a.m. on July 6, 1981, I received another dreadful call. It was Adam. Softly he said, "Hi."

It had been several days since I had seen him in the car with Rhonda. I thought of his face and the look of despair. I was glad to hear from him, but I was still very apprehensive.

I asked Adam, "Where are you?"

He replied, "I'm in jail."

I was not surprised. I knew the police were determined to apprehend the murderer. I started consoling him.

"Where are you being held? I will be right there."

I called Monica and told her the news. She asked me, "What are you going to do?"

"I am going to go see him."

"Okay, I will go with you."

It was a warm, dark, and silent night. I arrived at Monica's door with tears streaming down my face. We embraced, got in my car, and sped off to the police station.

I had never been to a police precinct. Monica and I found our way through the winding halls to the desk. I asked the desk sergeant if I could speak with Adam.

When I saw Adam, I immediately noticed his complexion had returned to its normal tone. He looked like himself. His eyes lit up within moments. We were both in tears. We cried together for a few minutes then regained our composure as best we could. A thousand thoughts went through my mind. How could my dream have come to such a tragic ending? How could my childhood friend, teenage sweetheart, husband, and lover for life be in jail for murder?

I was able to touch Adam through the cold iron bars. Overtaken with emotion, I got a chair and pulled it as close as I could to the cell. Adam and I talked openly and honestly for over three hours. I cried and cried.

Adam explained that a few days after the funeral, the police had come to the house where he and Rhonda were staying. They wanted to talk to Rhonda. They both went to the police precinct. They were separated for interrogation.

Rhonda told the police it was Adam who killed her mother. The police threatened him with the death penalty and promised him leniency if he confessed. Adam signed a confession.

Adam was charged with first-degree murder! He was in hell and I knew it. There is an old cliché, "confession is good for the soul," so Adam confessed his wrong and I knew he was remorseful.

He kept repeating, "I'm sorry."

Daylight quickly approached. Although I wanted to stay with Adam, I had to leave him sitting in that cold jail cell. I reassured him that I was going to stick by him through it all. But what was I going to do? I didn't have the first clue on how to handle this situation. I was bewildered!

I left the police station. I kept thinking, I have to go and tell our families this awful news.

My mother and father were not going to believe that Adam had killed somebody. I didn't believe it. Adam's mother might just die. She loved him very, very much. She had worked hard to build a home that was loving, safe, and nurturing for Adam and his brothers. He had been a good child, no arrests, no drugs, an A student, and she was proud of him.

I took Monica home so that she could go to work. She had known Adam almost as long as I had. She also loved him deeply. Monica was in disbelief about Adam, Rhonda, and the murder. She had insisted that I take a much more aggressive stand with Adam when his affair with Rhonda started, but I was too timid. I believe that my lack of courage stopped me from asserting the strength and power that I needed to conquer this ordeal. Although Monica did not like the way I handled Adam's affair with Rhonda, she continued to love and support me. She accepted my choices. I could not have made it through this tragedy without her constant love and support.

After dropping Monica off, I went home and called my daddy. I cannot remember our conversation. Everything was a blur. I only recall ending up at my mother-in-law's house. My father and I arrived almost at the same time. The sequence of events is hazy. I can still see us standing in a circle, holding hands, my father praying and crying. Adam's mother was frantic.

I worried I would collapse. At times I struggled to breathe. I managed to explain that Adam was in jail and charged with first-degree murder.

Only the three of us in the family knew the details. We still had to tell the rest of our relatives. Nobody was going to believe us. I dreaded having to tell this appalling turn of events to my family and friends. This was the beginning of a road I never imagined I would have to travel.

The news struck everyone like a bullet aimed at the heart. The wailing that came from my loved ones pierced the very depth of my soul. Family and friends embraced one another as the news spread of Adam's incarceration.

Nobody could believe that Adam had committed murder. Adam's mother retained an attorney.

During the next few weeks I was in a deep fog. At times I would cry uncontrollably. Other times I was so depressed I didn't want to do anything. My whole world came to an end.

The summer of 1981 was hell. It was August and I was approaching my twenty-first birthday. What I thought would be a good memorable occasion turned out to be the most tragic year of my life.

Although Adam had signed a confession, the pressure from our families forced him to plead not guilty and have a trial. No one in the family was ready to accept that Adam had killed someone. His lawyer told us that he would argue that the confession was coerced and that he hoped the court would throw it out.

I was waiting for events to unfold and I had so many questions. When would Adam have a trial? Would he be found not guilty? What if he is found guilty? Will they give him the death penalty?

I was trying to work and comprehend what was happening in my life. I was missing a lot of time from work. At times I wanted the trial to come quickly and then, at other times, I wanted it to never come.

My emotions vacillated between hurt, anger, depression, and fear. Some days I was mad as hell, other days I was confused and despondent. At times, it was too much for me to handle.

I was angry with Adam for getting involved with Rhonda. Everybody had heard of Rhonda's volatile relationship with her mother. Everyone thought that she was involved in her mother's death, but Adam was the only person in jail. When would the police charge Rhonda with murder?

Chapter 2

Solomon: I'm Trying to Cope

By the end of September 1981 I had lost my job because of the excessive amount of time I took off. Now, I was faced with even more time to ponder what was going to happen with Adam's trial. I had to make a change fast; otherwise, I would destroy my life. I had to start coping better.

I started the habit of going to two local disco clubs in the city, "Gatsby's" and "Odell's." They became my stress relievers. On Wednesday night, Monica and I would go discoing. Before Adam and I married it was a regular habit for Monica and me. Then it was just fun, now it was a way for me to try to forget all my troubles. I was raised in a family where music was significant. There was Motown and a song for every occasion. I played the piano and clarinet in elementary and junior high school. I have always loved music and it was now my vehicle of escape. When the music was playing, I felt no pain.

The pressure was taking me down, but I had a natural instinct for survival. I did not want to die from my pain.

By October I was working again as a legal secretary. I got the job through a temporary agency and now working was the only thing that made me feel normal. However, working did not take away the pain. I still felt that I had no reason to be happy.

On our second wedding anniversary, the disappointment was indescribable. I sat in my dark apartment crying and listening to Luther Vandross sing "A House is Not a Home." I never imagined celebrating our wedding anniversary with Adam in jail. My weekly visits with him did nothing to stimulate our relationship; they only kept alive the pain and agony of the reality that Adam could be in jail a long time. Adam still had not had his trial and the police still had not charged Rhonda with murder.

As the year was coming to an end I was still waiting — to wake up from my nightmare.

On a cold December evening, I was determined to go dancing. My car would not start, so I asked Uncle Joe if I could borrow his car. He lived only about a mile down the street.

Normally I would have walked, but it was too late for me to be walking alone, and it was cold. I decided to catch the bus to get the car. As I waited for the bus, a gorgeous black Trans Am drove up. It had a big gold eagle on the hood.

I recognized the car immediately. It belonged to Solomon, a guy who lived around the corner from me. I didn't know Solomon personally, but I knew of him, and I knew of his family. Solomon's youngest brother and my brother were in the same class in elementary school. Solomon's family was well known. They had a reputation for being very close and loving. Solomon's parents made an honest living and were well-respected owners of a successful day-care business.

He was a good-looking young man who had jet-black hair and a beautiful smile. When black men were sporting "big bushes," Solomon and his three brothers were known for having the biggest and prettiest bush.

Solomon and I had grown up in the same neighbor just one block away from each other, the same neighborhood where Adam and I grew up.

Solomon and I never played together while growing up. He was six years older. Now I was twenty-one and Solomon was twenty-seven.

Solomon pulled the car close to the curb, rolled the window down, and asked in a soft, sweet voice, "Would you like a ride?"

It was freezing outside, and I felt like I knew him. I said yes and jumped in the car.

We only had a short distance to ride before I reached Uncle Joe's house. Our conversation was very general and short.

Solomon said he recognized me and began to talk about my father's baby blue Cadillac with the name *Zollie* on the tag. He shared how he had admired the car. Solomon's father also had a Cadillac and his was yellow.

Back in the 1970s, black men called the Cadillac a "hog." I don't know why the car was referred to as a hog, but it was a symbol of achievement.

Immediately, I felt a connection with Solomon. Our families had similar traits and characteristics. I trusted his wholesome background.

As I was getting out of the car at Uncle Joe's house, Solomon asked if he could have my telephone number. Neither of us had a pen or paper so Solomon asked for my address. I didn't think he would remember it. I told him my address, got out of the car, and we parted with warm good-byes.

Although I was trying to cope, I was struggling with thoughts of Adam being incarcerated and the fate of our marriage. The anticipation of what would be the final outcome was tearing me apart inside. I was not happy with the circumstances of my life. I spent time doing anything that would prevent me from losing my mind. I continued to have a weekly night of disco dancing, my temporary escape from pain and confusion. My daily routine was blurred with pain and by the end of 1981 I knew I had to make some changes in my life. I needed a new beginning.

I joined a church closer to my home, the New Psalmist Baptist Church. Adam's mother had also recently joined the church, along with his two younger brothers, and we attended as a family. Having grown up as a Christian I knew the significance of having a place of refuge for talk and fellowship with God and other Christians.

On New Year's Eve, Monica and I spent the evening in church at Watchnight Service. Monica joined church that night and we vowed to make 1982 a better year.

I was so glad 1981 was behind me, although it had left an indelible memory on both my heart and mind that would travel with me for the rest of my life.

♥   ♥   ♥

In the middle of January Solomon paid me a visit. I was surprised when he showed up at my door, unannounced. He didn't have my phone number and I never expected him to remember my address. What I didn't know was that about five years earlier, Solomon had lived on the first floor in the same apartment building where I currently lived. What a coincidence.

Although not expecting him, I allowed him to come in to my apartment. I trusted him because of our neighborhood connection and his family's reputation.

Solomon was a machinist and worked in a chemical plant. He operated a large mixer of some kind. He was a blue-collar worker, just like my father, and he earned a good living. During this period, Baltimore was known for being a blue-collar town that employed thousands in the automobile and steel industries. Many of these Baltimoreans earned salaries that allowed them to live in the middle class so it was common for young men to graduate from high school and go to work.

Solomon's visit lasted about fifteen minutes or less. We sat on my couch and talked. I asked about his family and he inquired about mine. It was a short and pleasant conversation. After he left, I recalled that Solomon never took off his coat; nonetheless, I enjoyed the short visit. He was a pleasant man with a beautiful smile.

It was a cold, lonely, painful winter. Every night after work, I would listen to Luther Vandross's song "A House is Not a Home." I would listen to it over and over, singing along with Luther, understanding that the lyrics were real for me and I was living it.

> A chair is still a chair
> Even when there's no one sitting there
> But a chair is not a house
> And a house is not a home
> When there's no one there to hold you tight
> And no one there you can kiss goodnight. . . .
> Now and then I call your name
> And suddenly your face appears
> But it's just a crazy game
> When it ends, it ends in tears. . . .
> Are you gonna be in love with me?
> I want you and need to you to be
> Still in love with me!

My nights were agonizing. The pain of not having my husband home with me, but in jail. The pain of not knowing if he would ever come home to me was torturous.

As winter left and spring arrived, Solomon began to visit more often. His visits were always short and unannounced, but I didn't mind. We always sat on the couch and had a short conversation, often filled with laughter. Solomon had a great sense of humor. I enjoyed laughing with him and I wanted to forget that Adam was in jail, but I couldn't.

It was routine for me to visit Adam once a week in jail. Before Adam's incarceration I had never set foot in a penal institution. Visiting was a repulsive procedure where all the rules had to be followed, with correctional officers yelling to wait in line and remove all jewelry. The loud banging of opening and closing cell doors made me sick.

Adam and I could kiss and embrace only on entry and exit. We could not have any contact during the visit. If the rules were not followed the visit was terminated.

During my visits, Adam always tried to appear upbeat. We talked about the trial tactics he discussed with his lawyer and I tried to believe that he would be set free.

We talked about Rhonda, and Adam learned that she would be testifying against him. He had no response. We also talked about the shocking news that Rhonda was pregnant at the time of her mother's death with Adam's child. She later terminated the pregnancy. Again, Adam had no response. I don't know why he didn't have a response. But the look on his face was full of dismay. Maybe he didn't respond because he was also having trouble comprehending and coping with the turn of events that landed him in jail. For me, it only affirmed what I always believed, which was that Rhonda didn't love Adam. It was indisputable that Adam had sacrificed his entire life for someone who never loved him although she had proclaimed it many times.

After visiting Adam I was always sad and depressed for several days. I would have no peace.

At the beginning of the year I vowed to have a better year. So I made a commitment to myself to do better with managing my thoughts, emotions, and actions. I stopped my weekly disco dancing and I began spending more of my time in church. I needed clarity on how to move forward and because of my religious upbringing I turned to God for that clarity. I joined the choir and a Bible class. I tried to cope, one day at a time, with the goal of one day finding serenity.

Summer was coming and Solomon's visits were becoming more frequent and lasted longer. We sat on the couch, listened to music, and talked. I had all of Adam's stereo equipment and our extensive music collection. I enjoyed our music immensely. Often I would cry as I listened to the familiar songs to which Adam and I danced and kissed.

Solomon knew Adam and he had heard about the murder. We did not discuss the details. Sometimes, though, while we listened to music, I was unable to control my emotions and I would cry. Solomon never asked why I was crying. He would just say to me, "It's going to be all right." Slowly, I started to talk to him about Adam and what was going on with us.

At the end of his visits Solomon always gave me a warm good-bye. I discovered that Solomon had a gentle and witty personality. He was always joyful, humorous, and compassionate.

I felt that I was beginning to cope better. I was working and active in my church. I felt that I was ready to move forward with my life, but I really couldn't move forward because Adam was still in jail and still awaiting trial. It seemed that I had a big weight that was trying to pull me down and I was fighting to stay up.

In June 1982 Adam's trial finally began. I didn't know what to expect. Other than watching Perry Mason on television, I had no idea what the inside of a courtroom looked like.

In my mind, I tried to prepare for the trial. I kept telling myself that Adam would be acquitted and everything was going to be fine. It had been a year since the murder and I recalled the events of the last twelve months, regularly visiting Adam in jail and talking to him on the phone. It was a depressing experience! I could not comprehend how I could live like that, day in and day out, year in and year out. If Adam was convicted what was I going to do? I refused to think of the worst.

Adam's attorney asked me if I could testify on his behalf. Of course, I said yes. How could I not say something to help my husband?

♥　♥　♥

The trial lasted three days. I did not attend every day because I had been on my new job only a few months and had recently gotten a promotion. My life was becoming more stable, I was moving forward, and I did not want to jeopardize my progress.

The day came for me to testify. I entered the courthouse. It appeared dark and spooky. I took the elevator to the fifth floor. I began walking down the long corridor toward the courtroom. My feet were moving even though I felt like my legs were bricks. I was terrified. I could see my mother and mother-in-law seated on a bench at the far end of the hallway. As I got closer to them I noticed that they were shaking their heads, as if in astonishment. My mother approached me and in bewilderment she said, "I don't believe it. You and Rhonda are dressed alike."

I was wearing a navy blue dress with a big white collar and bow. Rhonda was also wearing a navy blue dress with a white sailor collar. We were all sitting in the hall together, waiting for the courtroom doors to open.

I was baffled by Rhonda's behavior. She expressed no emotion. I wasn't sure if it was because she was a strong person, or if it because she didn't care. I expected her to display some emotion because it was a trial about the murder of her mother.

She was pregnant and everyone could see her belly in the dress. Again I was shocked at how she appeared to be moving forward so quickly with her life. It had only been a year since her mother had been murdered, since she had terminated her pregnancy of Adam's baby and Adam had been in jail. Clearly she had gone forward with a new relationship, while I lay awake at night, crying and thinking about my husband being in jail for murder.

I felt tormented because I was questioning everything that I ever believed about love. I always believed that when you love someone you do not intentionally hurt them.

I thought Rhonda loved Adam. That's what she said while crying and begging to have him. Was it all a game?

Also in the hallway were the two detectives who had come to my apartment. The only seat in the small waiting area was on the bench next to them. I sat down. They were reviewing their file. As I glanced over, I saw a picture of the murder scene. I closed my eyes tight, tried to forget what I had seen, and moved away quickly.

The courtroom doors opened and everyone entered. As we were seated, Adam entered the courtroom. I paid careful attention to Rhonda and she never looked up at Adam. Adam sat down and opened his Bible.

Although the evidence came out that Adam had an affair with Rhonda I could not abandon him. I loved him deeply.

During my testimony I have no idea what I said. To this very day I have no memory of the judge, the prosecutor, or what questions I was asked. I only know I tried to talk about how wonderful Adam had been to me as a friend, his academic achievements, and his success in the Marine Corps.

Closing arguments concluded and it was over. Adam's fate was now in the hands of the jury. I returned to work and anxiously awaited their verdict. It was a crossroads in the fate of our marriage.

It was almost five-thirty when I finally received the phone call from my mother — Guilty!

After hearing the word, I dropped the phone, ran out of my office to the bathroom, and collapsed in tears on the floor.

Although Adam had already been incarcerated for a year, I still had hoped that he would be found not guilty.

I prayed that somehow he would not have to stay in jail long. We were still married. I wanted my husband to be free and to come home to me.

We can always have hopes and dreams, but the realization that they do not always come true can be devastating. Adam was sentenced to life. It was a fatal blow! He would have the right for the possibility of parole, but when? At the time, under Maryland law, a life sentence was considered to be at least twenty-five years. Would I have to wait twenty-five years to be with my husband?

It never crossed my mind that Adam would receive a life sentence. I thought the jury would see the good in him and have some leniency.

A life sentence could be forever. What was I supposed to do now? Is that what my wedding vow meant by "till death do us part"? As far as I was concerned this was death. I knew that I vowed to be Adam's wife through the good and the bad. I just never expected bad to be this bad. I didn't know if I could wait for Adam. What kind of life would I have being married to an inmate with a life sentence? No birthday parties, no anniversaries with romantic music and candlelight, no children. I pondered whether I should have to suffer because Adam decided to kill someone. My mind was flooded with questions and confusion.

Thankfully I was finding enjoyment in my new job and at my church.

Every Sunday that I went to church I kept waiting to hear God tell me what to do. I was trying my best to get my life on track. I had never imagined life without Adam.

Unfortunately, work, church, and the friendship with Solomon did not erase the reality that Adam was going to be in jail for a long time. I had to accept that what I imagined as marriage with him would never come to fruition.

Something inside me kept telling me to go forward with my life but I had no idea how. I was in bondage to my emotions. Outwardly I appeared just fine, but inside I was in turmoil and scared.

I continued my friendship with Solomon. I shared my feelings about Adam being sentenced to life. Solomon couldn't believe that Adam had received life in prison. Everyone remembered Adam as the quiet guy, the bookworm who didn't drink or use drugs.

I began to ask God to guide me. I knew that life with Adam in prison was going to be hell, for me and him. Doors clanging shut, correctional officers looking at your every move, restrictions on when you eat, what you eat, when you get visitors, and how long you get to visit. I was now fighting not to be angry with Adam. I didn't want to blame him but it was his fault.

I was having difficulty dealing with my life of regular visits to the penitentiary. I was always depressed after leaving Adam. I would miss time from work, stop eating, and have periods of uncontrollable weeping.

I questioned God because I did not understand why it happened. I prayed that I would survive because I didn't want to start sinking again. I had already lost one job when Adam got arrested. Now I finally had a new job that I enjoyed and I didn't want to lose it.

I was married but I had no husband. I wanted God to fix my marriage and get Adam out of jail.

I wasn't ready to get divorced and I wasn't ready for a serious relationship, but a relationship was all I ever knew. Adam and I were friends, Solomon and I were friends, and I started establishing some new male friendships. I always enjoyed the friendship of men. I had a great relationship with my father, my brother, my male cousins, my uncles, and my grandfathers. I loved all the men in my life. I had always desired to have the one special man, a husband, and now that was a broken dream.

It had always been easy for me to develop friendships. I am an extrovert and I have always found it easy to talk to strangers. I made male friends at work and at church. Whenever I met a man it always started with him asking, "Are you single?" It was the question that I dreaded because it was always the prelude to my saga. Men were always astounded by the story of Adam's incarceration.

For my benefit, God sent me some sincere, trustworthy male friends who supported me and encouraged me to be strong. They complimented me on my strength and love for Adam. At the same time, they encouraged me to get out and enjoy life.

Solomon was still slowly pursuing me, but I was not sure that I wanted to be in a relationship with him. I knew it would take a special kind of man to accept me and my past.

Back during my disco days, I met an older man who was eleven years my senior. Phillip was good looking and well groomed. He dressed impeccably. He was a ladies' man and somehow I became his lady. Almost immediately we developed a strong friendship that was built on respect and a mutual admiration for one another.

When I was depressed or scared, I would call Phillip. He would take me out for an evening. We would dine at expensive restaurants, shop at extravagant stores, and ride away in his sports car, which I adored. I fell in love with Phillip but we could not have a serious relationship because I was still in love with Adam.

Phillip tried to cope with my vacillating feelings for Adam, but my confusion always resulted in me doing something impulsive, like standing Phillip up because I was waiting for a telephone call from Adam in prison. I continued to get trapped in "what happened," and it hindered me from moving forward.

I thank God for Phillip because he entered my life during a most traumatic time and he tried to bring clarity and stability to me. I found solace in him. He was able to provide me with a secure atmosphere. He was older, stable, and he desired for me to be stable. He had a home, a good job, a nice car; he was intelligent and he had some money. He was a man of confidence and compassion.

However, my friendship with Phillip became a rocky road for him. I wavered back and forth between depression and optimism. I was desperately fighting to reconcile my love for Adam, his life sentence of incarceration, and my wedding vows.

Solomon was still visiting me and we had been out to dinner a few times. I was starting to enjoy our time together, but I was not ready for a committed relationship.

Slowly, it seemed that my marriage to Adam was coming to an end. I had Solomon as a friend and Phillip as a rescuer, but I still could not go forward to divorce him.

It was not until I met my friend Kenneth did I begin to change and move forward. Kenneth was fifteen years older than I and he too was well established. Kenneth was divorced and had two children. He took time to talk to me. We would talk for hours. He listened as I talked about Adam. He listened as I talked about Solomon and he would always end our conversations by telling me, "You need to fall in love with yourself!"

I had no idea what Kenneth was talking about. I did love myself. I told him I treat myself nicely, I buy myself nice things.

He said, "No, that is not what I am talking about. I'm talking about being in love with yourself."

At the time I could not comprehend what he was saying but I held onto his words, and slowly I began to make changes about how I thought of myself.

I remember buying a calligraphy set and writing on construction paper some words and themes to encourage myself. I wrote on one sign the words "I'm on my way to the top one step at a time." I drew a ladder beside the words and I taped the sign on my bedroom wall. Every day I read it, several times a day, and slowly I started to feel myself changing, just a little at a time.

I changed my focus from thinking about Adam and his incarceration to thinking about me and my life. I kept hearing Kenneth's words "fall in love with yourself." My question was, how?

When I asked Kenneth how, he replied, "You will know when it happens!"

Over a year had passed since Adam was sentenced to life in prison. I would still visit him in jail, although my routine of once a week had dwindled to twice a month. I knew I couldn't go on with the jail visits having to recall the nightmare over and over. There was no happiness in my jail visits. Just trying to accept the circumstances was a job in itself. The fact that Adam was in jail serving a life sentence was a reality that I continued to struggle to accept. It was painful seeing him behind the barriers of prison. It appeared that the more I tried to go forward in accepting that my husband was in prison, the more it seemed that I would slip back into despair and disappointment.

I spoke with my pastor and my parents. My pastor was clear in letting me know that the Bible did not condone divorce. My parents did not want me to be divorced — our family didn't believe in divorces. I did not want to be divorced. Divorce was looked upon as failure. It was a hard choice, but I decided I would divorce Adam because I was determined to begin to build a new life for myself. I could not keep stumbling through each day, not giving any thought to my future. Although I made the decision to divorce Adam, I was not ready to deal with the stigma of being divorced so I didn't file right away.

I tried to maintain a routine of things that made me feel good. I went to church and work, socialized with my friends, and Monica and I did a little partying. I spent time with Solomon, went to dinner with Phillip, and listened to Kenneth tell me to fall in love with myself. I had only one problem: I was still in love with Adam. I never knew trying to stop loving someone was so hard.

Trying to cope with the pain of losing the relationship was almost fatal for me. I masked my pain with pretty clothes, shoes, and jewelry. I have always enjoyed dressing fashionably and looking nice, but it was only an outward appearance. I felt a hole inside me that was big enough to destroy me.

I wanted what I thought was normal, a good marriage.

Solomon and I began more serious dating, without formally giving our relationship a title. I discovered that he was romantic and full of charm. He was a good family man with a loving and close family. Solomon is the oldest of four boys. I was excited when I met his parents. I fell in love with them almost immediately. They welcomed me with open arms into their hearts, home, and family.

I also introduced Solomon to my family. He was definitely a gentleman. My family came to love Solomon, his charm, his compassion, and his ability to always make people laugh. My family treated him just like a son.

I felt myself being more attracted to Solomon. I knew it was because of the closeness I observed in his family which resembled my family so much.

Family values are a foundation for my character. Solomon and I were raised with the same family values. We both enjoyed family gatherings.

I was still very close with Adam's mother and his family too. We all still attended the same church and I still attended family outings.

By June of 1983, my visits to Adam had become more infrequent. It was sheer torture to even think about going to see him in jail. My family saw my pain and they were adamant that I move on, but that was much easier said than done. I never wanted to sever my relationship with Adam, but it was becoming more and more difficult to live with his being in prison. I slowly began to spend less time with Adam's family and more time with Solomon and his family.

What I really wanted, I could not have. I wanted to be married and I had to accept that my marriage with Adam was over.

It was another sad and disappointing summer.

For my twenty-third birthday I drove to Ocean City to watch the sunrise. I cannot say why I was compelled to go to the ocean, except I have always loved nature. I have always been intrigued by the essence of how nature operates without intervention from man. The sun coming over the horizon and night turning to day seemed symbolic of what I was trying to do in my life: turn darkness to light. I knew that I needed clarity because my goal of being a wife and mother had been torn out of my arms. I had no marriage, no husband, and no children, the very things that I had always aspired to attain. But even without them I was determined to find serenity in my life.

I had grown to love Solomon, Phillip, and Kenneth. I desired a committed relationship with somebody, but who? I could not move forward holding onto the past with Adam so I finally started the divorce proceedings. It was one of the saddest visits I had with Adam. I was working for a law firm as a paralegal at the time, and I told Adam that my boss would be handling the divorce. He said he understood that he caused me so much pain. He also said, "Princess, I do not want to lose you." I assured him that I would always love him, that we would always be friends, and that I would always keep in contact with him. I told him how I felt when I left him, crying and depressed. I told him that I had to start thinking about my future. He said, "I understand, I will sign for the divorce." In July 1983, my divorce from Adam was final.

♥   ♥   ♥

I enrolled in the evening division at the University of Baltimore to complete my undergraduate degree. I always enjoyed school and had some career goals but they were only secondary to being a wife and mother. Now I had to set a new goal for myself. So I started to use education as a means of self-fulfillment. I was starting to enjoy a new aspect of my life.

I wanted the focus of my life to be something other than a relationship with a man, but that was what I thought life was about — being a wife and a mother.

I was young, naive, and immature in so many ways. I was starting to feel what "growing up" means. I was faced with emotions I had never felt and decisions I had never considered.

I continued to date Solomon and gradually I noticed that there were changes in his personality when he had been drinking. Solomon and his friends enjoyed drinking socially. He was six years my senior and about to be thirty. I was only twenty-three and didn't really drink, maybe a glass of wine every now and then. What I noticed was that I did not like Solomon when he had too much to drink. He was much too aggressive in his speech and his actions.

Solomon knew that I had other male friends and he did not voice his opinion until he had something to drink.

One night when Kenneth was at my apartment, Solomon stopped by, unannounced as usual. After learning that I had a guest, he went outside. Suddenly, a bottle crashed through my apartment window. I knew Solomon had been drinking.

I dismissed it because Solomon was a good man, possessing good basic characteristics. He was a good-hearted person, sincere and honest. Solomon's drinking wasn't all that bad; after all, my father drank and my mother handled it. I thought I could too because Solomon loved me and I still believed that love was enough to conquer any obstacle.

Kenneth cautioned me about Solomon's behavior but I ignored the warning. I knew that Solomon cared for me. I should have expected Solomon to react the way he did. He was very possessive and, when he was drinking, sometimes his jealousy would show.

Phillip and Kenneth were still my friends and I knew that neither was ready for marriage. Marriage was a commitment that neither of them was ready to make. Also, I was afraid my father would think they were both too old for me, so I never saw them as anything but friends. Even with their friendship my goal was still to be a wife and a mother.

On October 31, 1983, my paternal grandfather died. He was my first grandparent to die and I wrote a poem for my family, entitled "Nothing Remains the Same Forever." It was a lesson I had to learn.

> Nothing remains the same forever.
> Winter comes and winter goes,
> Children are born and children die.
> Nothing remains the same forever.
> Remember the smiles,

Remember the tears,
Remember the good times through all the years.
Love is eternal to be passed on and that which is given
should be handled with care,
For nothing remains the same forever.
People are gifts given to us — only for a short while.
But memories go with us — until the end.
Nothing remains the same forever.
As each day passes remember one thing,
Life will not last and death will come.
Create a memory that reaches to heaven,
A smile for those who love you — to carry in their heart.
Nothing remains the same forever.
No — nothing remains the same forever.

I was starting to discover that life is not always pleasant, easy, or predictable. I wanted to be successful in my endeavors and I wanted to have a fulfilling life with a husband and children, but how?

The end of the year was approaching and once again I was determined to be content and happy. So I started writing in a journal. It was my first survival tool, helping me get in touch with my feelings, my disappointment, fears, and anger. I knew I had to organize my thoughts. I wanted to understand why I felt the way I did and I wanted to feel better. I wanted to feel good about myself and my life. As I started making entries, I discovered that I felt relief when I wrote. It became a source of strength which allowed me to open up to myself, and to be honest with myself, about my emotions.

I discovered that some days I could not face my thoughts. I was afraid to look at myself. I didn't like what I saw: pain in my heart and confusion in my mind. My emotions were too great and I was too weak to confront them, so I wouldn't write in my journal. But I learned to conquer my fears and overcome my doubts by acknowledging my pain. It took time but I later realized that I did not have to be ashamed of my pain.

My journal entry usually started with me acknowledging God. It was like my prayer. I would then begin to write about how I was feeling at the moment, or how I felt earlier and how I wanted to feel later. I closed my entry with a motivator, a proclamation to fight on, to conquer and succeed in my quest to be happy.

I would always review the prior journal entry before making a new one. By reviewing the earlier entry, I was able to see how I was coping and I was able to see my ability to persevere, and how I was relying on a strength that I knew came only from the God that I serve.

I can recall reading over some of these entries and experiencing strong feelings of happiness and, sometimes, strong feelings of sadness as my eyes would fill with tears. My mind would travel back to the events that captivated my heart, mind, and soul. The road I paved allowed me to travel from fear and despair to courage and tranquility.

When I began my first journal I remember thinking, "You've got to keep yourself together." My life had changed quickly and drastically, and it was only by the strong hand of my Almighty God that I survived.

Deep inside I knew that I had to motivate myself to get past the past. My first journal entry was the beginning:

December 29, 1983
Today I purchased this book and the thoughts and ideas will mold me to be the woman that I am meant and want to be.
Theme: "I Shall Rise Above It All"

It made me feel good just knowing I wanted to rise above my past, but how? Although I was in school and stable in my employment, I still had a desire to be married.

I considered all of Solomon's good points. He was trustworthy. During the entire two years that we dated I never had any reason to suspect that Solomon was dishonest or cheating. Solomon had a good job, he was kind and romantic. Solomon adored me and tried his best to give me my desires. Solomon was a strong family man from a Christian family. I told Solomon I wanted to get married and we began discussing it. Solomon had never been married and had no children.

I discussed it with my parents and they advised me to wait. They loved Solomon but for several reasons they said, "Wait!" Mama told me I was not ready and neither was Solomon. I did not want to believe her because I thought I had to start my dream of marriage over again.

I was only twenty-three years old and I wanted a husband and children. I wanted us all to live happily ever after — that is what the love music, movies, and every romantic novel is all about. I thought this was the right track for me.

I was hurt that my family was not agreeing with me. At times I was impulsive and would make one hasty decision right after another. For months I purchased only purple clothes and shoes. My family could not understand why everything I wore had to be purple.

I cut off all my hair and wore what I described as a little-boy haircut. My hair was close to my head like a boy's. My mother was furious with me. Women did not wear short hair during this era, but I found joy in wearing my purple clothes, and I found courage in wearing my short haircut. I was discovering me!

Solomon and I set a wedding date, his birthday, December 27. As I made preparations for our wedding, I received unsolicited advice from the people who loved me. Some said, "He is a real nice guy but you should wait to get married." During this time the last thing I knew how to do was wait. I still wanted to be married and I did not want to wait. I wanted to be a wife and a mother.

Many of my family members began praying for my guidance. A maternal second cousin told me that God told her that I should not marry Solomon, that I was making a mistake. I resented my cousin for being so bold with her opinion. I tried to dismiss what I heard, although I couldn't.

I began to pray seriously. Since a little girl, I have always prayed and had conversations with God, most of the time never listening, but definitely talking. I told God how I was feeling. My belief tells me that God is all-knowing, so God knew I could be hardheaded and strong willed. And, if it was not meant for me to marry Solomon, then I needed a big red sign.

Monica also knew Solomon. I asked her what she thought. She was still single and I trusted her opinion. She agreed that Solomon was a good man who loved me.

I said to God, "Lord, even if it's on my wedding day, if it is not meant for me to marry Solomon, then don't let my legs move." They were words that would come back to haunt me.

On December 27, 1984, Solomon and I were married. Solomon's mother was elated. He was her first son to marry.

The wedding was gorgeous. It was an evening wedding and the church was beautifully decorated in the spirit of the Christmas season. It was a cool, crisp, clear night. The stars sparkled on the velvet background of a black sky.

I was dressed in an elegant ivory tea-length gown. I loved it even more than my first wedding gown. Excitement was in the air, but I was scared to death.

The groomsmen were dressed in stunning black tuxedos and the ladies were dazzling in red satin tea-length gowns.

The wedding began. Parents and grandparents had been seated, the bridal party marched in, and it was now time for me to make my grand entrance.

Without any warning, my legs felt as though they were in two blocks of cement. I tried to step into the foyer of the church but I could not move. I then spoke softly to my father and wedding coordinator, "My legs won't move." Those haunting words from my prayer came back to me.

My father and wedding coordinator ran to my side. They both began to comfort me, they told me to calm down, everything was okay. I began to drag myself into the church. Even with the assistance of my father I was barely able to walk. I thought I would never make it down the long aisle, lined with beautiful red rose petals that lay softly on the white runner. My father held my hand tightly and literally carried me down the aisle. It was from that point I knew I had made the mistake of not listening. Yet, I kept a smile on my face, and hid the fear in my heart, hoping and praying that God would make everything fine.

The first morning of our marriage was a disaster.

We had plans to travel to the Pocono Mountains for our honeymoon. Solomon was fully aware of our plans, but he failed to prepare for the trip. He had not packed and he had not prepared the car. I was so mad and hurt. I began crying. Disappointment in my marriage seemed to have become my lot in life. I told my parents, who were at the apartment, to leave and I wanted Solomon to leave. My mother politely said, "We can leave, but he stays, that's your husband. Remember?" She began to shake her head. As I continued to cry, she said softly to me, "I knew this would happen, but I didn't think it would be this soon." It was my first brush with the reality that I had made a mistake. Clearly Solomon was not prepared for the responsibility of caring for a wife. Solomon was a carefree man, who never had much responsibility beyond making a car payment and paying rent.

Solomon had no debt and a good job, but he gambled with his money, socializing, drinking, and having a good time. I knew all of this before I married Solomon but I overlooked it and did not give it much significance. I only knew we loved each other and that was what was important.

Unfortunately, I was in a fog when I made the very critical decision to get married a second time. I was still in love with Adam and still fighting within my own mind and heart to understand the path for my life.

Solomon and I went on our honeymoon, had a good time, and came home to the real thing. It was business as usual. Solomon worked swing shifts and often we would not see each other.

I was still in school and regularly involved in my church. Solomon continued to be irresponsible and misuse his money. I became very frustrated with my condition and I resented myself for being in this situation. I knew that I was still trying to cope with my loss of Adam.

In my mind I could still hear Kenneth: "Fall in love with yourself." I kept searching, even though I didn't know what I was searching for and I didn't know where to look for it. I was trying to find in Solomon something that could only be found in myself.

Solomon and I began to talk about our problems. He approached the subject with very little seriousness. I asked him to make some changes. What a request to make of someone! What I know now is not many people break habits without determination and willpower. I wanted Solomon to change, but he was comfortable with his lifestyle and I realized I had no right to try to change him.

Nonetheless, Solomon promised he would change. He did make some attempts, but nothing really changed. After it was clear to me that nothing was changing, I began to think about changing me.

I started thinking about leaving Solomon. I knew I had to get out. I was suffocating in my own pain. Solomon was irresponsible and that only frustrated me. Adam was still in jail serving his life sentence, and I was on marriage number two and still no children. My dream of a happy marriage was once again falling apart. I started feeling like I was losing my mind. I did not know what to do!

Thankfully, I had maintained my spiritual relationship with God. I talked to God and to myself more than ever. I attended church regularly. I was committed to my ministries at church, but it was painful being there too.

Divorce was an uncommon ugly thing in the seventies and eighties and the church did not like it. I knew people at church were whispering and talking about me being married twice and I wasn't even twenty-five. I knew that people at church had made judgments about me and my circumstances, without knowing the facts. But I ignored what I knew they were saying, and instead I listened to the words of my pastor and through him I began to hear the voice of God, inside of me, become clearer.

I had heard God speak encouragement to me before, but now I began to gain strength. I began to hear God telling me that "He would NEVER leave me nor forsake me." It was a scripture that I had read and recited but this was the first time I embraced it.

I enjoyed going to my church. I love the high praise of God through music and song. I love my gospel music more than any of my tear-jerking, slow-dragging, finger-popping, and booty-wiggling jams. I love gospel music because it is inspiring and powerful, filled with great words of the promises of God, penned to the harmonious sound of instruments. In church the music would grab me as I sang the words of Walter Hawkins's "Oh Happy Day." In church I would shout, cry, scream, and I would run. My church was the environment for my emotional release and my spiritual empowerment.

People in church would look at me, not knowing the full magnitude of my internal trauma. They only knew I was divorced and now remarried without children.

Nevertheless, I found in my church a comfort in God that I had never known. When I was a child my mother taught me the 23rd Psalm. I learned to recite it early in life and now I was using the 23rd Psalm to live with peace and joy every day.

Marriage with Solomon was a struggle. I was getting tired of his nights out, drinking, and gambling. I asked Solomon to leave if he wasn't going to change his habits. Much to my surprise, he said he would leave and I accepted it. However, he made no attempts to leave and he kept doing the same things.

I had noticed during our discussions about separating that Solomon would become aggressive with me. I began to look for an apartment without his knowledge. I found a serene apartment about fifteen miles away on the other side of town. The apartment had everything I wanted. It was beautiful. Set in a valley of oak trees among a magnificent landscape created only by God, this place was where I knew God intended for me to be.

Without any notice to Solomon, one evening after work I rented a fifteen-foot U-Haul truck. I drove it home and packed my belongings, which was a chore because nothing was ready. My brother, his girlfriend Kattrina, and I packed for three hours. Monica joined us about ten thirty and finally around eleven thirty we had finished packing everything in green trash bags. It was a green trash bag horror.

Solomon arrived just before we left. He was so hurt and so was I. When he walked in I could see the pain in his eyes. I never intended for it to be this way. We loved each other.

I left and as I drove away, I cried, asking God, why?

We separated only seven months after our beautiful wedding.

I arrived at my new apartment about one o'clock a.m. and finally around four my new apartment was filled with over thirty big green trash bags. I was energized by the change because I knew I needed some space and time to be by myself. I thought, finally I have some peace.

I loved the area known as Ellicott City. For the first time, I was thrilled to be by myself. The next day I awakened to the green trash bag nightmare and methodically began to tear through the bags.

After a few hours of unpacking I looked out my balcony doors. I observed a car coming down the driveway. As it got closer to my apartment building I noticed that it was Solomon. I feared what might happen. As he drove up to my apartment building I started thinking, what am I going to do?

Solomon got out of the car, walked into my building, and knocked on my door.

How did he know where I lived? I never told him I was moving.

I hesitantly opened the door. I thought it would be safer to let him in than to have him embarrass me by screaming in the hall.

When he came in he sat down looking sad and hurt. He began uttering hateful words to me, saying, "You will never be anything" and "You ain't shit."

I told him, "I want you to leave." I was afraid he would become more aggressive. I knew he had been drinking and the alcohol could certainly change his character. Although I knew that Solomon would never intentionally physically hurt me, his words were hurting me and the pain was excruciating.

Our marriage was falling apart despite the love that we shared. It was not enough to keep us together. We were both hurt and disappointed.

After a few moments and the utterance of more obscenities, Solomon hesitantly left. I watched him through the window as he walked to his car. But he didn't get in the car, he looked in the trunk of the car. Solomon pulled out the jack for changing the tire, went over to my car, my brand-new Toyota Corolla, and he proceeded to smash the windshield, then the driver's side window.

I calmly picked up the telephone, called the police, and watched Solomon destroy the windows in my car.

After speaking with the police I called my daddy. Again, it was Daddy to the rescue. My father dropped everything and came to help me. He gave me one of his cars so that I could get to work the next day and he took my car for repair, with the broken glass in millions of little pieces all over the seats and floor. My father reassured me everything would be fine. He kissed me and said, "I'll take care of everything."

The police located Solomon driving just a mile or so from my apartment. They did not arrest him and I did not pursue charges against him. I knew that Solomon was hurt because I had left him. I knew that he loved me and I knew that he wanted our marriage to work, and so did I. I learned from Solomon that he got my address when the rental agent called the apartment to verify information. I had no idea that he knew I was going to leave him.

Solomon and I agreed to stay away from each other. I began to try to put my life in order. I was determined to fall in love with myself.

I began working in Washington, D.C., as a legal secretary with a very large law firm. It was ranked fourth largest in the United States. It was plush and ritzy and I was so happy! Finally, I had a great new job, I was enjoying my apartment, and I was coping with my divorce from Adam and my separation from Solomon.

I enjoyed working in the legal profession and although I had still not completed my undergraduate degree I now knew that I wanted to be a lawyer.

I loved my job as a legal secretary. It gave me great satisfaction. The firm had over eight hundred attorneys worldwide and they were rich. It was an elite firm with the smartest lawyers in the country. The pay was outstanding. I enjoyed commuting to Washington and, for the first time in five years, I felt like I was making progress. Slowly, I began discovering more about myself.

Although I was discovering myself, I still had not found real love with myself. I still desired to be a wife and a mother. I recall the pain I would experience when I saw couples. I would stay away from places where couples would go, like the movies. It would make me feel so sad when I would see a couple, holding hands, laughing, kissing, and just enjoying each other. It was what I had desired so much and yet it had eluded me.

Ironically, right across the court from my apartment, there was the most loving couple.

I would watch them come and go, together, holding hands, laughing, smiling, and sometimes kissing. He owned a little sports car and he treated her like she was a queen. I remember for some special occasion he pulled up in a chauffeur-driven limousine, he got out with roses, went to the door, and escorted her away. I wanted to absolutely die. It was a picture of sharing and caring. It was love as I always envisioned it and I had it and I lost it. And I still desired to get it again.

I was not enjoying the dating scene, and clubs were no longer my cup of tea. I was growing in new ways, yet I still wanted to be a wife and mother.

I moved to a bigger apartment within the same complex, and this one sat higher on the hill above the valley of oak trees. The view was spectacular!

I bought all new furniture and I began to discover more of me.

I was finally beginning to be comfortable with me but I never lost my desire to be a wife and mother, to love and be loved. My passion for love was still deep inside of me just like the blood in my veins, and yet it eluded me. I was unable to unleash it and allow it to grow with the one person I always desired, a husband.

I constantly went through it in my mind, over and over again. First I would think about Adam and our strong serious childhood love that blossomed and died. I couldn't stop thinking about Adam, the murder, and his life sentence in prison. It haunted me like a cloud in the sky.

Then I would go back and forth in my mind and heart about Solomon, his drinking, his irresponsibility, his kind heart yet volatile nature, and his sincere love for me. I traveled around in my head trying to find a reasonable explanation for why I was now married a second time and now separated. I did not like it and I did not understand it!

I stood out among my peers. None of them had been married twice already. Monica was still single. My friends at church were still single. It was agonizing being different. I was glad I had conquered some of my fears of being different by still wearing my short haircut, which was now my signature.

For the next few years I stabilized. I had a good job, a very nice apartment, a church family that provided me with a great place for fellowship, and, of course, the continuing and unconditional love of my family. I had made some progress from the depressing and tearful nights of 1981, but I still had the desire to have a happy marriage and to be a mother.

It was the fall of 1986. I was lonely and still married to Solomon. We had not spoken in months. I wanted some companionship so I called Solomon. It was like we had never split up. He said he was happy to hear my voice and I was happy to hear his. We talked about how each of us was doing and we both apologized for the mistakes that led to our separation. We agreed to start seeing each other to work on a reconciliation.

It was never my intention to abandon my marriage to Solomon. I always wanted us to be together, but why did circumstances have to interfere and complicate matters?

The next thing I knew, we were back together. Solomon was living at my apartment. We did not spend a lot of time discussing what happened; we got back together and started moving forward.

I was attempting to live up to my vows. I knew Solomon and I loved each other. We were married and we were on again. Everybody who loved us was happy.

My in-laws and I had always shared a loving relationship and we just picked up where we left off. Solomon's three brothers were always my brothers and we all loved each other. We shared a very close relationship regardless of the circumstances between Solomon and me.

I was acting out what I learned from Mama and that is love never ends! My grandparents separated when I was about six years old. I do not know the circumstances, but what I do know is that one day I realized that my grandfather no longer lived in the house with Mama.

As a young girl, I would often listen to the family discussions around the kitchen table. Sometimes it was just the women: Mama, my mother and her two sisters, and me. If the conversation got too mature for me, I was told to leave the room. I overheard that Papa was living with another woman, Ms. Alberta. Mama said Ms. Alberta had a lot of children, that Papa had made a mistake, and that he would be sorry that he left.

It didn't appear to be traumatic for anyone. There was no screaming and no crying. Our Sunday family dinner routine continued and life seemed to go on as normal, but Papa just didn't live with Mama anymore. He was still Papa, and Mama never said a bad thing about him.

Eventually Mama met a male friend, Mr. Kelly, and he became a part of our family. It was another event that our family adjusted to without any drama.

Throughout my life, I observed my mother and her sisters continuing to support and love their daddy. I recall us going by Ms. Alberta's house and visiting Papa.

It was easy to love him even though he wasn't living with my Mama because everybody else still loved him and they showed it, especially Mama.

Mama never visited Papa where he lived with Ms. Alberta, but she did communicate with him and Ms. Alberta with some frequency. Mama would call Ms. Alberta to give Papa messages about the family and what was happening in North Carolina.

Papa and Ms. Alberta had one child together. Papa's only son, Carmichael, was much younger than my mother and her sisters and, although they acknowledged him, there was no regular interaction between them.

Papa would sometimes have a holiday dinner with us. I observed my grandparents being cordial and polite with each other. When it was time for Papa to leave after a holiday dinner, Mama would always fix him a big plate to take home — enough for him, Ms. Alberta, and Carmichael.

I never observed Mama being angry or disrespectful with Papa. Mr. Kelly lived with Mama, and he and Papa were cordial too.

We were all one family and we all loved each other, with all our flaws and the mistakes that people make in life.

Solomon and I were living together again. We had both matured, a little, and we were experiencing fewer problems. Solomon had cut down on his drinking and gambling. We both worked. I was still in school at night and we enjoyed time together with our families. I was still involved in my church ministries, but Solomon did not attend church with me, and I accepted it.

Our reconciliation was good. Solomon and I shared a peaceful and joyful marriage during this time. We discussed having a baby. We both wanted children. Solomon was elated about the prospect of being a father. So we tried. Monica was pregnant and my brother's girlfriend, Kattrina, was pregnant. So it was perfect — we would all have babies around the same time.

I began to think that Solomon and I were going to be a family. It was now possible, I was more secure in myself, Solomon was more disciplined, and our sincere love for each other was certainly a recipe for our success. I felt we had a solid foundation and, thankfully, nothing was happening to shake the foundation.

We started searching for a house to buy and setting goals for our future, but something wasn't right. I could not put my finger on it, but inside I felt something was still missing although I desperately wanted to believe that all was well.

I was now twenty-seven. I had matured, I was gainfully employed, matriculating in college, active in church, growing in my relationship with God, yet I knew something was about to happen. But what?

It had been several years since I had spoken with Adam and I surmised that our relationship was finally behind me.

It was January 8, 1988. It started as a rather odd day. It was the dead of winter and there had been a blizzard in Maryland with over four feet of snow. Everything was closed, from the federal government to churches. Solomon and I were home and I planned for us to enjoy the day off and relax. At nine o'clock, we were still in the bed, preparing to watch one of my favorite television shows, the *I Love Lucy* show. The telephone rang; it was my father.

Daddy had recently taken an early retirement on the advice of his doctors. He was diabetic with ensuing complications. I was concerned about his health, especially since he was still drinking, but I put it in the back of my mind. I couldn't imagine anything happening to my father. I loved him so very much.

We talked casually about the weather and my car needing some repairs. Daddy told me, "Wait until one warm day and bring me your car and I will put the brakes on for you." Our conversation ended as usual: "I'll talk to you later."

I went on with my day, relaxing with Solomon and enjoying being off from work. Later in the evening Solomon and I got out of the house to get some food. The snow had stopped falling and the roads were being cleared. There were huge mountains of snow along most roadsides. It was a winter wonderland.

Solomon and I returned home about seven and shortly after we got in, Kattrina called. She sounded strange and immediately asked me if I had spoken with my mother. When I told her that I had not, she said, "You should call your mother right away."

When I called my mother and asked her what was wrong with Kattrina, Mommy softly replied, "Baby, Daddy is dead."

I screamed and threw the telephone across the room. Solomon came running frantically to my side. I remember Solomon talking to my mother and asking, "What is wrong? What happened?"

Everything went blank. The next thing I remember was the police arriving at my door. They had received a call about someone screaming. Solomon told the officers that I had just been informed about the death of my father. I was in shock!

After a while, I gained some composure and called my mother back. I asked her what happened. I thought that maybe it was a heart attack but I was flabbergasted when she said, "Daddy was hit by a car while crossing the highway."

The police had come to the house and told her that Daddy's car had stalled in the snow, and he was crossing the highway to get to the telephone booth.

From that moment, my life changed forever. A part of me died.

Solomon and I packed a bag and went to my mother's house. The next few days were filled with lots of tears and little to no sleep or food. Every day hundreds of people came to pay their respects and offer their condolences. It made me sick to have to greet them. It was certainly kind of them to come support us, but with every kind word spoken about my father, it caused my heart pain. It was surreal.

Solomon and I left my mother's house the day before Daddy's funeral to go home and get clothing. I remember crying profusely and saying to Solomon, "How do I figure out what to wear to my daddy's funeral?" With each breath my chest hurt, my mind ached, and my heart was cracking into tiny pieces. I wanted somebody to tell me I was dreaming. I remembered my last conversation with Daddy and knew that day in the spring would never come.

The pain was deeply penetrating into my soul. Before this, everything had been going along smoothly. Solomon and I were together, I was still in school and only twenty-one credits away from my undergraduate degree, my employment was sound, my spiritual foundation was solid, and now another unexpected, traumatic event. I felt lost.

I was shaken like an earthquake had hit. I told my mother that I was not going back to school, and I didn't know when I would go back to work. She prayed with me and continued to pray for me every day, believing I would come around and go on with life.

Everybody who knew how very close Daddy and I were began to worry if I would recover and nobody worried about me more than I did. Could I survive? I had never imagined that I would have to live without my father.

Other relatives of mine had died but this was my daddy and I couldn't understand how I was going to live without him.

Again, I felt that I was being forced to let go of someone I wanted to hold on to. First, it was the divorce from Adam and now, it was Daddy's death. Again, I wasn't getting a choice in the matter.

How do you let go of what you want to keep? I had no idea. The question seemed illogical, because why consider letting go of something you desire to keep? I was tormented by my lack of understanding how I should cope.

I struggled to accept that Daddy was gone, never to be seen again. Every day I cried out to God for everything, for strength, for joy, and for a desire to live. I needed it all to get up in the morning and face a new day.

I went back to work but I was not the same. I needed something that I felt I didn't already have. So I drew closer and closer to my God because I believed He had the answer. I found just what I needed and I found it in a deeper relationship with God and His word. Again I used my love for music to help me cross over. The main chorus of a gospel song was "If you're looking for LOVE, John 3:16 — He loved the world He gave his only son; JOY, Nehemiah 8:10 — The joy of the Lord is my strength; SALVATION, Psalm 27:1 — The Lord is my light and my salvation; PEACE, Isaiah 26:3 — I will keep you in perfect peace." I played this song every day on my way to and from work and it became a bridge that I used to cross over from despair to hope.

On one hand I was gaining strength and slowly finding peace in living without my father; nonetheless, on the other, my life was not joyful and pleasant. I had to learn how to smile again. Even though I had lots of reasons to smile — I was healthy and I still had the love of my husband, family, and friends — my pain seemed to overshadow everything that was good. One of the reasons I used to smile was now gone. My daddy was a big, big part of my life and even though I knew that he would someday die, I never wanted it to happen.

I fought every day, emotionally and spiritually, to get back on track. After much encouragement from my mother, who told me, "Daddy would want you to finish school," I returned to college. Mommy told me that Daddy was now my guardian angel.

I registered for school during the last week of late registration. The registrar told me, as she looked at my course selections, "You will not get into these classes; you are too late."

The registrar went to the computer, put in my selections, turned to me in astonishment, and said, "You must have an angel looking out for you. You got into every class!" It was my sign that Daddy and God wanted me to proceed, full speed ahead, even though I didn't want to go full speed ahead. My pain was deep and I was struggling to find strength to overcome.

Solomon was also grieving the loss of Daddy. He would constantly say, "I can't believe Daddy is gone." He also began to drink more often. I was doing everything I could to keep myself together. I found it difficult trying to cope with his pain and my own. I needed some help and, at this time, Solomon was not equipped to give it to me.

I had so many questions for God. Why? Why now?

I had not spoken with Adam for several years. I thought our relationship was finally behind me, but I was wrong. He called me from jail the day after Daddy died. His mother obviously told him. I was still in communication with my mother-in-law and brothers-in-law. We all still attended the same church and, more importantly, we were still family and loved each other.

I was glad to hear Adam's voice. My mind flooded with a thousand memories, good and bad.

I knew Adam was also grieving, and his grief was complicated by his incarceration. He did not have the comfort of the people he loved most to surround him. He told me he felt guilty because he was not around to comfort me during this very difficult time.

Adam asked if he could call me again and I said yes.

Although Adam was incarcerated, his mind was still free and growing, and I still trusted him. I knew that he knew of my sorrow and he told me to draw closer to God.

I told Solomon about Adam's call. He didn't seem to mind. I guess he figured that Adam was in jail and no threat. Plus, Solomon was also consumed with his own grief and trying to find his way.

Adam began calling me with regularity. Like old times, I enjoyed our conversations. Adam's words were encouraging and soothing to my painful heart. Our conversations always included prayer and a scripture for me to meditate on.

Adam also wrote me letters filled with encouragement. I always felt better after reading one. It seemed that he understood what I needed, and once again we began to rekindle our connection.

I attempted to have a normal life. It was not easy. I was trying to cope with my emotions, which at times were uncontrollable. I could be happy one minute and in the next full of despair.

On Saturday, April 9, 1988, I was driving my car to be serviced. I began to cry profusely as I thought of my last conversation with Daddy. My eyes swelled with tears. It became difficult for me to see the road, so I pulled off to the shoulder.

It was a cloudy, gray day. I stopped the car and allowed myself to weep, and in my weeping I heard God say, "Look up." I knew it was God because I have regular conversations with Him and I recognize His voice. When I looked at the sky I saw a hole in the clouds; it looked like an eye into the heavens.

I immediately took out a pen and paper and began to write what I heard God saying to me. I wrote the words in a poem, and my words describe what I saw and how I felt. I entitled the poem "Look UP."

The sky was full of clouds

God moves the clouds in masses

O what a mighty good God we serve

But I looked beyond the clouds

There was a rainbow that surrounded them

As the sun shined bright, you could see heaven.

The harder you looked, the longer you looked, the brighter it got.

My Father is there and He looks down on me

with a smile that shines so bright

I looked up — way over the clouds and I know

He looked at me.

Oh praise be to God. I shall forever look up!

From that day I have looked up at the sky every day. From this experience I became a sky watcher! Every day I looked up and sought guidance. It helped, but I still hurt!

Not until my father's death did I realize how much I could miss a person's voice. For months I grieved because I just wanted to hear my daddy's voice. I wanted to feel the pleasure of hearing him call my name, but it would never happen, and I had to accept it.

I knew I had to go forward. I was trying my best. I was still trying to put the present and the past in perspective. I was still trying to accept the things that I could not change. Adam was in jail, I was divorced, and Daddy was dead.

I enrolled in a program at my church designed to help develop spirituality and, once again, I began to diligently read and study the word of God. It was the only source of strength I could rely on.

My desire to be content became a priority!

It was May 1988. I was still in anguish and each day was like a torturous journey to survive. Adam was still writing and calling me, with regularity, and I was still finding comfort in his encouragement. However, as comforting as the conversations and letters were, our communication now only added to the complexity of my thoughts and confusion.

Solomon's drinking was now excessive. I knew he was grieving and although I wanted to help him, I couldn't. I was still trying to help myself and not drown in the sorrows of life.

Once again, Solomon and I began to encounter marital problems. He and I were together physically, but we were apart emotionally and spiritually.

On Memorial Day, Solomon and I decided to celebrate with Monica, Monroe, and their new baby, Bethany. I was still not pregnant.

We gathered at Monica's apartment and decided to get some crabs, a tradition for Baltimoreans. We were drinking beer, eating crabs, and having a good time, when suddenly things changed!

I was discussing a recent magazine article with Monroe, and Solomon disagreed with my opinion about it. As best I can recall, it was nothing of great significance but, whatever it was, Solomon became very angry.

I knew he had had too much to drink, and the fun quickly turned into screaming and cursing. What happened? I know that I have strong opinions and I find it easy to articulate my thoughts, but this was crazy. Everything I said to defuse the situation irritated and enraged him.

Solomon began yelling, "You think you know everything." I was shocked. I thought it was just the alcohol, but it went deeper.

He belittled me, telling me I wasn't shit. I was being attacked. As Solomon spewed his nasty, hateful words, I heard the voice of evil say to me, "Cut his throat and shut him up." I went to the kitchen and reached for a knife.

My emotions were already convoluted, with Daddy dead, Adam in jail, writing and calling me, and Solomon still drinking. Everything was so confusing now.

I was disappointed that Solomon was unable to relate to my grief, although I knew he could and I knew he was still grieving, but never did I expect him to turn on me.

Thank God Monica closed my hand in the kitchen drawer before I could reach the knife.

At this point I knew things would never be the same for Solomon and me. This was the culminating event. I knew I had to move away from him. It was dangerous for me to have such overpowering anger and hurt. Without thinking, I could go to jail for doing something I would regret forever, just like Adam.

Things went from bad to worse. Not only was I grieving Daddy's death, now my second marriage was in big trouble.

I wanted to die but couldn't. Something deep inside me was keeping me alive and it had to be in my faith in God!

Monroe took Solomon for a ride, and I dashed to my car and rushed home. I had no idea what Solomon was thinking and I was afraid of what might happen if another argument started. I called my rental office and told them I needed my locks changed right away. I explained that I was afraid of my husband, who was not on the lease, and he had a key to my apartment. They changed the lock.

I packed Solomon's things, and called Monica and told her to let him know that I did not want him to come back and I would make arrangements to get his clothes to him.

This time I knew Solomon and I would never reunite.

Once again, I was disappointed and hurt that my story-book tale of living happily ever after was not fulfilled, and it only exacerbated my already painful existence.

I was not ready to begin the dreaded process of divorcing. I did not want my marriage with Solomon to end. I never expected marriage to be perfect. My parents shared a loving relationship and it was not void of problems and trials. I watched them maneuver through their trials and provide my brother and me with a stable and loving home. So why couldn't I do the same? That was my expectation!

But I knew Solomon and I had to part or someone might get hurt. Solomon obviously felt the same way because he never tried to reconcile after this separation.

I felt myself fighting for my life, believing I was making a good choice, but feeling dismayed, confused, scared, and bewildered. I pressed on.

I believed that God had something special for me and I was determined to get it. With every ounce of strength that I could muster, I kept seeking understanding for my life.

At this juncture I decided to go forward with my aspiration of becoming a lawyer.

In August 1988 I graduated with my bachelor's degree from the University of Maryland. Finally I had accomplished my goal. I was now ready to move on and I was headed for law school.

It was Labor Day weekend. I thought my life was heading on the right road. I was in North Carolina for our annual family reunion. I was visiting with one of my second cousins, Uncle Nitty, who was not just a cousin but a father figure, someone whom I trusted and respected deeply.

My first morning at his house with him and his wife, we were having breakfast and Uncle Nitty asked me how I was doing. He knew the trauma that was in my life. He knew about Adam, Solomon, and my grief for Daddy's death.

I wanted to act like I was handling things well, but I couldn't fake it. I told him I was hurting and I was talking to Adam again and that it was making me feel better.

I'll never forget Uncle Nitty's face. He looked across the table and sternly said to me, "You will never be stable if you keep going back."

When he spoke these words it was like thunder! It was then that I finally made the decision to let go of my emotional dependency on Adam. I was compelled by Uncle Nitty's admonishment to put to rest my broken dream of being with Adam.

For years I had held that broken dream in my mind and heart. It haunted me and, at last, I let it go!

After returning from North Carolina I stopped all communication with Adam. It was not easy but I knew God was guiding me and I began to release myself from the emotional attachment.

Like a raging fire, I began pursuing my goal to be an attorney. I studied for the Law School Admission Test. I put all my time and attention into it. This was not an easy goal to achieve. I knew law school was competitive and my first step was to get accepted.

I was now determined that nothing would stop me from achieving my identity. I desired to be a self-sufficient woman. I desired to be content and satisfied with myself, by myself.

I vowed to love myself always and to love myself the best. It was now a ritual for me to make my annual trip to the beach to watch the sunrise in August for my birthday. I didn't need anybody to go with me because I love nature and have always found enjoyment with it. It was fun and peaceful sitting on the water's edge, watching the sun come over the horizon like a fireball out of the sea. I watched in amazement as the horizon went from being dark and subdued to bright and exhilarating. I was in awe. I took this time to think, reflect, and set goals. It was another survival tactic for me. Watching the sunrise allowed me to gain clarity. Being away from the noise of the city and the distractions of work and family helped me to focus on myself.

Much to my astonishment, I discovered that marriage, a husband, and children were no longer my priority. I now desired to have a successful career and I wanted to be a lawyer. Also I was having some problems with fibroid tumors and since my career had taken priority over motherhood, I decided to have a hysterectomy and forever abandon my desire to give birth. I felt it was for the best.

Solomon had accepted our separation and did not contact me. We agreed that we loved each other but it was best that we not be together. In September his grandmother died. He called me and I attended the funeral. I loved Solomon's grandmother, and I was deeply saddened by her death. Solomon and I talked about death and how it was impacting our lives, and embraced. It was clear to me that the love between us was sincere, and although we were not together we still loved each other.

I was still grieving Daddy's death but I could feel myself getting stronger. Every day I would look up at the sky for guidance, comfort, strength, and peace. I was making progress.

In November all seemed well. My first niece was now nine months old, and she was the jewel of our family. Her birth brought new life to us all. She was born at the end of February, just seven weeks after Daddy's death. She was the sunshine that we all desperately needed. Once again life was moving forward, and things were getting better.

The day before Thanksgiving, the phone rang and it was my mother. She said, "Uncle Joe has died."

Uncle Joe was married to my mother's youngest sister. He was such a wonderful man. He had a smile that lit up a room like a spotlight. I was the flower girl in their wedding. I lived with them for two years after graduating from high school, before Adam and I got married. I loved Uncle Joe deeply. He did anything he could to help me. He washed my car in the summer, sometimes every week, and he made it shine like a diamond. He was a kind man with a big heart and I was devastated again. Since Daddy's death, I looked to Uncle Joe as my father figure.

What my mother said was outlandish. How could Uncle Joe be dead? Again, I thought I was losing my mind. But I knew I had to keep myself together. I asked God, "What is going on?" Daddy was dead and now Uncle Joe too.

Uncle Joe had gone into the hospital for minor surgery and never awakened after the operation. Another unforeseen tragic event that life was forcing me to face! In a fairly quick succession God allowed some of the most significant men in my life to leave me. I did not understand why!

I went through the next few months striving to live and not die, trying to put all the pieces together, questioning God over and over, why? Some people believe that you shouldn't question God. I have never had that belief because the Bible tells us to ask. The Bible tells us to seek, so I have never had difficulty seeking answers from God. Unfortunately, during this time, I was not receiving any answer to my questions. But I didn't give up on God giving me the answers; I just didn't know when the answers would come.

It was difficult times again, but I used what I knew. I used my knowledge of God and His power. I trusted and believed that things were working out for my good, no matter how bad it looked. I trusted and believed that God would never leave me nor forsake me. I was excited about the development of my relationship with God. I was still very active in my church, which was thriving under the leadership of my anointed pastor.

I was taking one day at a time and I worked to become a confident and more mature woman. My days were filled with working and going to church. I felt stronger, and I was moving in the right direction.

I promised myself that I would not be distracted by love ever again. I thought that I should stay far away from love. It was just not the best thing for me, although it was the thing that made me smile the brightest. I was scared to get hurt again and I vowed to protect my already broken heart.

I did not date. I would occasionally go out with friends but my focus was on loving God and loving myself.

I vowed to make myself first in my life and never to trust my heart again to love. I vowed to think rationally about my choices. If I ever chose to love again, and at this time I thought that was doubtful, I vowed to be a strong and independent woman.

Finally, I began to travel my road to self-fulfillment. It was not easy. I was doing alone what I had always believed would be shared with a husband. Nonetheless, I began to put the past behind me. I vowed to remain single and forge ahead as a successful attorney, secure and satisfied with self. But something happened!

Chapter 3

David: A Surprise?

At the end of 1989, I was twenty-nine years old, financially secure with a good-paying job, single, no children, married twice, divorced once, separated, and learning to love myself.

I had adorned my apartment with new furnishings more befitting of my evolving personality. I changed from a home for my husband to a home for me. I used shades of pink and my favorite color, purple. I had a few credit cards, and I filled my walk-in closet full of clothes, too many to wear, so I became accustomed to seeing clothes hanging in the closet with the tags still on them. Of course, shoes, shoes, and more shoes. A lady can never have enough shoes, my new philosophy.

I have always loved jewelry, but diamonds are my favorite. I received my first diamond as a gift from my father, for my fourteenth birthday. It is a beautiful gold charm, designed as a bell with the clapper holding a small diamond chip. It is not worth much, nor is it big and fabulous, but it was my gateway to a fascination with and love of beautiful diamonds.

I still owned my wedding rings from Adam, so I traded them in and purchased myself a stylish diamond ring. I still had my wedding rings from Solomon. They were specially designed for me by my jeweler. They were a symbol of our devotion, but I knew it wouldn't be long before I would trade them too. Now I had another new lifestyle, and I made sure my hands glittered with the fire of diamonds.

I was still working as a legal secretary in Washington. It had now been five years and I had discovered a new and exciting world in D.C. I was discovering life beyond being a wife. I felt good about it all. I was discovering more about me, what I enjoyed and what I disliked. I was captivated.

When my grief for Daddy would strike me, I would look up at the sky, smile, and keep moving forward.

I filled my evenings with activities I enjoyed. I took advantage of the spectacular dining experiences in Washington.

It was strange learning how to enjoy a meal alone. I would walk into a restaurant, the maître d' would say, "Hello, seating for how many?" I would respond, "One." Initially, I would get a look of surprise, then I would be ushered to my seat. I wondered, "What do people think?" At first it was uncomfortable for me but, over time, I learned to love it. I developed the tranquility of being alone. I learned to enjoy ordering my meal and the satisfying taste of my food! I had learned to enjoy dining out alone and being comfortable being alone. It was another survival tool.

It had been seven years since my marriage to Adam had dissolved into a nightmare, but in that time I made progress. I was no longer the uncertain, scared, and confused young lady who had difficulty coping with disappointment. I had matured into a young lady who, through adversity, obtained courage, perseverance, self-fulfillment, and peace. My pastor had watched me over the years. Although I knew he did not condone my divorces, I also knew he was proud of me because I had triumphed over my circumstances, which surely could have defeated and killed me.

Every year our church had what was called the "Bible Institute" which was an array of classes designed to have a positive influence on every member of the family. I was asked to teach a class for single women, entitled "Saved, Single and Satisfied." The objective of the class was to instill life skills in women who were single that would enable them to be content. When I shared with the women my habit of eating out alone, many said, "I can't do that." "That's no fun." To me those words and those ideas were chains of bondage and a hindrance to self-fulfillment. I learned fun is what I make it!

When I did not want to be alone I was fortunate to always have a friend who was available to spend some quality time with me. I regularly spent time at concerts in the parks. I embraced the phenomena of nature. I began my childhood ritual of collecting rocks again and I placed them all around my apartment. They are my symbols of strength.

For the first time in my life I was beginning to enjoy my time, with myself, being single.

I would spend all day on Sundays at church. I was in the choir and the usher board and involved in teaching new members. I loved it all.

I was loving my job in Washington, D.C. I was loving my apartment in the woods of Patapsco State Park.

I was still enjoying my music. I would reminiscence with the Temptations, Otis Redding, Al Green, and the Bee Gees. I would recall all the fun times I had listening and dancing to their beats with my loved ones who were no longer present in my life. It was overwhelming yet refreshing because after the tears there was always a smile. Such great memories live in my mind.

I was eager to get started with my goal of becoming an attorney. I had graduated from high school over twelve years ago. In some ways I felt I was just a little behind in pursuing my higher education; nonetheless, I was enthusiastic and ready to go.

My divorce from Adam and my separation from Solomon had left me feeling very cautious. Although I knew in my heart that one day I had to love again, I began to make some adjustments in my mind about love.

First I stopped thinking about me and a man. Instead, I started thinking about me. Me and only me, although deep inside I still felt a small tugging at my heart, to be in love again, and to get married again. I wanted to put that thought in a box, lock it up, and hide the key.

Divorced once and I was now headed to a second one. Solomon and I had not seen each other or talked to each other in almost a year. I had heard he was confronting some problems: no job and too much drinking. Nonetheless, I still loved him but I knew our marriage had no future. I was not even the same woman he married. I had grown and matured in ways that separated us. I had a new dream of becoming a lawyer, and being a wife was no longer a dream. Although I still believed that I would someday have a marriage that would last, a marriage that would last longer than a few years, I stopped making it my only dream. I now had some dreams for myself.

I was overcoming yet still fighting. I was developing a "new attitude," as Patti LaBelle sings, but I was also battling the stigma of being a divorcée, both in my family as well as in my church.

During the 1980s people who were divorced were still stigmatized and, in many circles today, divorce can still have a stigma.

My family did not condone divorce. At the time, no one in my maternal family had been divorced, except me. My Mama and Papa had been separated for close to twenty years, and they were still married. In my paternal family there was only one divorce, an uncle's, and now I was number two.

I had to overcome my own mother's embarrassment of my divorces. Whenever the subject came up with friends or family and I would say that

I wanted, one day, to get married again, my mother would quickly reply, "Oh, no, please no more weddings and no more invitations." I understood that she didn't understand why I had to be divorced. For many years I couldn't believe it either, but I was learning to accept my lot in life and often I would just laugh.

In my church some people would whisper and look at me out of the corner of their eye. I knew they were curious about why I was divorced. I surmised that many thought that my marriages were "failures," but I kept my head up because I knew I had not failed. I could have stayed married to Adam. He would be in jail and I would visit him and devote my life to his imprisonment. I still could have been with Solomon. He may have consumed too much alcohol, but we still would have been together. It was a choice and I did not consider myself a failure because I chose to divorce.

This was another internal battle that was significant in my overcoming what people thought about me. I was determined not to let other people define how I felt about myself. I certainly did not feel like a failure and I certainly did not feel like my marriages were failures. To me, nobody was at fault: there were circumstances that we could not overcome together, and I was learning that in life we all have limitations and our limitations do not make us bad, weak, or failures. Learning to articulate that principle and helping other people to understand it has taken many years, especially when people have such strong opinions about marriage and divorce. However, I was determined not to live my life by other people's beliefs about me or what I did or didn't do. I was learning to be independent in thought and I relished the process.

I was satisfied with myself and every part of my life. I had just applied to the University of Maryland School of Law, and I was eagerly awaiting my letter of acceptance. I was sure that I would get accepted. Before I graduated with my undergraduate degree, I would drive slowly by the University of Maryland law school. I would gaze through the library window, observing the law students studying, and I would hear the spirit saying, "One day you are going to attend this law school." I had great expectations of doing just that!

I also had a special reason for wanting to attend Maryland's law school. Justice Thurgood Marshall's denial of admission into the school inspired me to cross the threshold and go where a prominent black man had once been denied the privilege of attendance, a man who fought so hard for equality. For me it would be poetic justice. He was a source for my own determination to be successful and to overcome barriers that could block my way. I thought of how every day I would walk through the halls thinking of Justice Marshall and how he must have felt and how he never let it deter him from succeeding. I felt in my spirit that it was destiny!

At last I was developing my spiritual intuition. I was astounded by the discovery. In the past I did not consider my choices carefully and sometimes I was too quick to make a decision. Now I was thinking, waiting, and praying before making a move. I was excited with the revelation that I was developing life skills that I would benefit from forever. During this time I began to rely on my spiritual-intuitive voice and, whenever I heard it, I would say, "It dropped in my spirit" to do this, or, "It dropped in my spirit that I should not do this." It became a powerful tool and I maintained my belief that love is the best thing in life.

In December 1989, Raymond, a friend from church, asked me to attend his anniversary to celebrate his sobriety. He was free from the abuse of alcohol and drugs. I had met several people in my church who were recovering from the abuse of drugs and alcohol. I was humbled by their struggle to overcome such a strong force as addiction. I thought it could have been me and I admired my friends for conquering what seemed to be insurmountable for so many.

It was at this anniversary that I met David. It was held in a small room with about twenty people. Some were seated while others walked to and from the coffee machine. This was a first for me. I observed and listened to the speakers.

I was not looking for a man. I had found security in my singleness and courage to accept that I was single and not married. I had come to love me and trust myself. I was no longer afraid of making a choice, thinking I was being compulsive or impulsive. I had developed a sense of who I was and who I was becoming and it felt real good!

I finally knew that I was in love with me.

Raymond introduced the next speaker; it was David. At first glance I saw David as another man with issues and I was staying away from men with issues. I watched David as he walked to the podium to speak. He was a very good-looking man and I don't mean just good looking. I mean fine, six feet four inches tall, beautiful hazel brown eyes, a big pretty smile, and a body that could put Denzel Washington to shame. But his good looks were no big deal to me because I was past the "fine" syndrome. I was clear that looks do not define a person's character and their propensity to be honest and trustworthy, so I just looked and dismissed him from my mind.

After the anniversary David and I both attended a small gathering at Raymond's house. During the evening David and I began to have some casual interaction. I observed him as he talked and laughed with friends. I listened to his comments about his life, his struggles, and his goals. I saw in David traits that caused a curiosity in me: perseverance, faith, and determination. They were all strong characteristics, ones that I also possessed. I was a little intrigued, but again I dismissed him from my mind. However, I gained a deep respect for him and his tenacity and ability to overcome.

I was feeling an attraction.

When the evening was coming to an end, I said good night to Raymond and his guests. Coincidentally, David also began to walk toward the door and say good night to everyone. Without any planning from me, David and I left at the same time. We walked out the door together and parted ways at the parking lot with good nights and warm smiles.

As I pulled off, I noticed that David was behind me in his truck. I thought, just another coincidence. Then we came to a red light and David pulled his truck beside my car, rolled down his window, and asked me if he could have my telephone number. I said yes, and we exchanged numbers and parted ways.

I was thrilled to feel my heart beating again but I was clear that I was not looking for love. I was determined to make sure he knew that, because I was headed to law school and was not looking for a relationship.

♥   ♥   ♥

Another new year arrived: 1990. Solomon and I were still not together and we were not even trying to reconcile. I thought that we should divorce, but I was not ready, not yet, not again!

As the year got started, David called, and slowly we began to share the stories of our life. I disclosed to him the horror of my divorce from Adam and my separation from Solomon. He disclosed to me the pitfalls that he had experienced in life. He had four children and was in his first year of recovery from drugs.

Initially, I was hesitant about forming a friendship with David. I did not want to be distracted from my goals nor did I want to lose myself to someone else's trials.

After several days of phone conversations that lasted for hours, David asked me out for dinner, and I accepted.

David was burdened by bad choices but, as I spent time getting to know him, I began to admire his strength and his will to never give up. I was intrigued.

David was not a scholarly man. He had only a high-school education; however, although I was headed to law school, this did not deter me from spending time with him.

David was employed as a carpenter. He had outstanding skills. He could turn a dilapidated room into a luxurious suite. David was also an entrepreneur, building his own home improvement business. He worked long hours, sometimes seven days a week. I applauded his stamina.

I was still working in Washington and waiting to start law school. For the first time in eight years I felt stable.

David and I began to share our deepest fears and doubts with each other. We would talk for hours about our emotions, our choices in life, the consequences of our choices, and our dreams. He became one of my best friends. His ability to communicate honestly about his feelings was exceptional. I was astonished by his deep level of communication. He never hesitated to articulate how he felt, either good or bad.

He was honest about himself and the mistakes that he had made with women. It was clear to me he had issues with women or women had issues with him. I could see where any woman who looked at him would think he was fine, I want him. But there is always more to it than meets the eye and, at this stage of the game, I was still hesitant about him and a relationship with him.

In March we began seeing each other frequently. I could feel myself developing feelings for him. He also loved music, just like me; he was romantic, just like me. We enjoyed candlelit nights, soft music, some dancing, some laughter, a little kissing, and always some real good food.

I saw independence in David. I saw strength in him. I saw that I could be myself with him, and I enjoyed the relationship immensely. It was easy and gratifying for me.

We would go to church together and that was a plus, especially since neither Adam nor Solomon had attended regularly. It was something that I longed for in a relationship.

During playtime we went to the park, rode bikes, attended musical concerts, and dined out regularly.

I felt my life was on the right track and, finally, I had let go of the past and my future looked bright.

In June Solomon and I divorced. It was not an easy decision for me to divorce a second time but I knew that Solomon and I were never going to reunite; we had already tried twice. Solomon obviously felt the same way, because he did not fight the divorce. We both accepted that we loved each other but we could not make it as husband and wife. It is so sad but it's the truth. I learned to accept the truth, no matter how much it hurts, because truth is both freedom and power. When you have the truth you have the privilege of knowing and the option to respond. I believe truth is a cornerstone of wisdom.

Even though I never expected a second divorce, I had to accept the reality that my marriage to Solomon ended in one. I received the divorce decree in the mail. It was a somber day that left me feeling a little perplexed because I still loved Solomon. Other than that, the process was uneventful, just as it was with Adam. Uncontested, no bickering, no disputes: just me and a witness and it was over. Unbelievable! In my mind, the process was too quick. In some cases, it took years to get from dating to marriage. My weddings took months to plan and the divorce took fifteen minutes. It was certainly too fast to come to an end to what was intended to be for a lifetime.

In August of 1990 I entered the University of Maryland School of Law. I was ecstatic!

At last, I was on my way to achieving my goal of becoming an attorney. I resigned from my job as a legal secretary in Washington although I had not saved a penny, but the attorney I worked for advised me that I should attend full-time. I used my faith and gave up my apartment, sold my furniture, gave things away, and moved in with my mother. No one was at the house with her now that Daddy was gone and my brother was living on his own. There was plenty of room. Being in the house without Daddy was depressing, but law school kept me busy.

Law school was demanding. Seven days a week, every week, for at least sixteen hours every day. There was reading, reading, and more reading. It consumed me, and my mind, all my time, except on Friday night. David and I had a date night and it was every Friday night. It was a welcome relief from the law books.

While attending law school, I felt David's support. He encouraged me to be the best I could and never complained about me having to study all the time.

David was also very busy, with fifteen- and sixteen-hour days. He was diligently working two jobs to build his business. It seemed that our lifestyles were perfect for each other.

The end of the year was approaching, and I began to sense a stronger attraction between David and me. I looked forward to our time together, and I was enjoying my life. Sometimes I thought I should run away from the relationship because I knew I was falling in love with David. I had vowed to stay single and not get married and my past routine had been to fall in love and get married. I was afraid.

My new rule was no marriage, and I was dedicated to keeping it as the rule. Although I was pursuing a prestigious career, which required dedication, I kept my dream for marriage hidden in the secret place of my mind and heart. I wouldn't talk about marriage, and I wouldn't think about marriage, but I had not forgotten about marriage and how important it was to me.

My dream for children was gone forever and, when I considered David's life, that was perfect because he didn't want any more children.

Although I had a new rule, I started developing more feelings for David. I started thinking about whether I could get married again. It had not been a topic of discussion for David and me. All of our conversations had been only about my marriages and divorces. David was empathetic as he listened to me describe my heartbreaks. At the end of each conversation he would reply, "I want to get married one day."

The first year of law school was ending and I thought, at last a break.

David and I were still dating and it was getting serious. We spent all of our free time together. I met his mother, grandmother, sister, and his children. We attended family events together. I knew we were in love. David wanted to get married and I was considering breaking my rule. On numerous occasions, we discussed our past and the decisions we each made. During each conversation, David spoke eagerly of his desire to be married. I began to consider marriage again because of his desire for marriage and I was in love with him.

David wasn't really sure that he was ready and I wasn't either, but we kept talking about it and praying about it. I did not want to make another mistake, so I tried to move slowly and cautiously.

My second year of law school was beginning and although living with my mother presented no problems for me, I wanted my own place again. It would not be easy to get my own apartment because I was a full-time student and unemployed, but I wanted to. I had come to love the power I felt having my own home and being in control. There is something very liberating about having your own, knowing that it is yours and under your full control.

So I transferred to the evening division in law school and got a job working as a law clerk in the general counsel's office for a corporation located just a few blocks from the law school. It was perfect!

I told David that I was getting my own apartment and he asked why I needed to do that, weren't things fine with us? I told him that it had nothing to do with us, that things were fine with us, but I wanted my own. David was not an insecure man, but he knew other men were interested in me. He often joked about Raymond, the man who introduced us, and how Raymond wanted to be with me. I assured him that my decision had nothing to do with him or any other man. However, having my own apartment was a sign of independence and David did not want me to be too independent. I believe that every man wants his lady to depend on him, to some extent, no matter how successful or independent she may be. Maybe it's a form of possessiveness or maybe it's just the nature of a man to want to provide for his lady. I knew David did not want to take a chance on losing me and I didn't want to lose him because we had a very good relationship. My decision was about me making sure I was looking out for myself and not falling into my past and looking for a home with a husband.

I believe David and I both were trying to proceed with caution and awareness, but the next thing I knew, David said he was ready to get married. He told me that he had enough of the single life and was ready to settle down. At first I was startled because I had one thought in mind — single lady, bachelorette pad again — but I could not dismiss that David and I were in love, and love took first place.

We talked about our expectations, our hopes, and aspirations for our life. David asked me to be his wife, and I said yes!

Now I must admit that although David said he was ready, to me he still appeared ambivalent. I tried not to dwell on his ambivalence because I had my own fears. Some days I felt like I should get in my car and drive far away, as fast as I could. However, I believed that David was the right man in all ways. We shared so many similar characteristics: we were both people of faith, independent, aggressive, confident, good communicators, romantic, honest, and loving.

Why wouldn't it work? We loved each other and we were best friends in every sense of the word. He called me his "partner."

My mother thought I was crazy when I told her that we were going to get married. I expected her response because she still had not come to accept that I had been married and divorced twice. I had done something nobody in my maternal family had ever done. My mother did not like it because divorce was not something our family did. I knew that she was afraid that I was making another mistake, and she didn't hesitate to tell me. I just listened and still went on with planning my wedding. My mother will tell you that I am a very strong-willed person. When I set my mind to do something, usually nobody can talk me out of it. My mother knew this, so she just voiced her opinion knowing that it would probably not cause me to change my mind.

Although I had charted a single life for myself, marriage was still at the core of my heart. David was ambivalent, I was afraid, yet our love for each other and our desire to be married trumped our fears. After dating for seventeen months, David and I were married on July 26, 1991.

My third wedding was nothing like the first two. There was not a huge fanfare. No wedding gown, no invitations, less than thirty guests, no bridesmaids, only a matron of honor, and no groomsmen. It wasn't even at a church. The ceremony was held on a Friday evening in a small banquet room at our best friend's condominium. I was blessed to have my godmother perform the ceremony in the company of our immediate family and friends. The reception was held in the same room. Although it was small — all we could afford — it was cozy and intimate, and I was satisfied. I thought maybe it will definitely work now. My father had always said that people who have those big weddings never stay together. Although I knew that wasn't true, I had two big weddings and neither marriage lasted. Maybe there was something to it?

After getting married, David and I continued to work long hours. David would often leave home at six-thirty in the morning, and I was out the door shortly after him. David would return home around ten at night and I would arrive minutes after him. I enjoyed our intense work schedules, and I felt that we were working on our goals for our life.

We had a fun, loving marriage. David liked to laugh and so did I. We would play around the house together, singing and dancing, kissing and hugging. I was so very satisfied. I doted on David, and he doted on me. He showered me regularly with flowers, romantic cards, and candlelight dinners. We continued our Friday night date with passionate lovemaking, with thoughts of joy and dreams that it would never end. It was our time together; he stopped working and I stopped working and studying. We continued this practice throughout our marriage as if we were always courting.

However, David did have some trouble adjusting to his role as a husband. He now had responsibilities to a wife, and his past followed him, like a shadow. He had four children with three women.

Our first year of marriage had a few rocks in the road. This was my third marriage and David's first and we were in what I call the merge crisis, when two people, with some similarities and some differences, merge to form one union.

I found that many couples have their worst troubles within the first two or three years of marriage. Adam and I separated after eighteen months. Solomon and I separated after seven months of marriage. I didn't have a good track record for surviving the merge crisis but I was determined that David and I would make it.

I started believing that if I could only make it through the first two years it would last. I was determined that this marriage was going to work. This would be the marriage that would last until death do us part.

I encouraged David to spend time with his children and to cultivate a better relationship with their mothers, but it was hard. His oldest daughter's mother was now very sick. She had used drugs for most of her life and was dying from its complications. His second daughter's mother hated him, and it was clear to me that the two of them would never have a good relationship. I encouraged him to stay close with his daughter despite her mother. His two youngest children's mother was on the fence. She wanted him to be a responsible father but she always resented that she and David were not together, especially since she stood by him during his many years of drug addiction. Again, I encouraged David to be the best father he could and routinely made sure the kids spent time with us.

David and I got through the first year of marriage. We prayed together, and we attended church together regularly. We were determined not to give up, no matter how tough it got.

The second year things got better. David and I enjoyed our life together. Our home was harmonious, filled with all the things we both loved: a clean neat environment, good food, lots of music and movies for our entertainment. We were good together. He understood me, and I understood him. We adjusted the rough edges of our personality and we were fitting together. People could see our genuine happiness.

We developed a circle of married friends, couples who were also working on their relationships, finding joy in being together and overcoming the stumbling blocks. We would often gather and talk about the "marriage thing." The men had their opinions and the women had theirs. After an evening of hearty discussion, everyone left laughing and hugging, feeling satisfied. It was great.

I loved to entertain and David enjoyed it with me. We never needed a special occasion. We always had friends over for dinner, cookouts, and parties. Life was absolutely blissful.

The support and encouragement that I received from David through-out law school was heroic. He comforted me when I stayed up, for nights at a time, studying for exams. He rallied with me when I received my grades. He was my best fan. When it came time for me to graduate, David was more excited than I was about the ceremony. I was going to skip the graduation. I was thirty-three years old and thought the ritual was no big deal. David, however, insisted that I participate, and I am thankful that he did. It was one of the greatest days of my life.

I graduated from law school in our second year of marriage. During this time the legal profession encountered a drastic turnaround. The sav-ings-and-loan crisis put a strain on the profession and, for the first time in decades, lawyers began to experience widespread unemployment. There were not enough jobs and too many lawyers. It was frightening in some respects but I relied on my God. In the past I had always been blessed to find a job and, once again, I trusted God to lead me in my search.

The marriage frontier was looking great. I was studying for the bar exam and I was expecting my career to blast off. Then sickness attacked the person dearest to me.

Starting in the early summer of 1993, Mama suffered three strokes within a three-month period. Again my world felt the tremors of life.

At first everything seemed okay with Mama. I thought she would make a full recovery; however, within a short period of time she lost her ability to talk, walk, and do anything for herself. Life was very different.

Inside I was distraught, but I tried to hold myself together as best I could. Mama was my hero and I had to watch her slowly die. I was in disbelief!

As the days and months passed, Mama never regained mobility nor was she ever able to speak with any clarity. I continued to visit regularly, but instead of her cooking for me, now I fed her through a straw. I missed hearing her words of wisdom, her thoughts on situations and circumstances. I wanted her back the way she used to be! It was my job to give her a manicure and a pedicure. I made sure I kept her fingers and toenails looking pretty, the way she always did. Her debilitating state was hard for all of us. Mama was the anchor and we all relied on her advice. I knew it was hard for her, too, because she loved to talk to us, and she loved to prepare meals for us. Each day with her I treasured while at the same time dreading the inevitable, for which I was unprepared. Mama was my sweetie and as her only granddaughter I maintained a special role in her life. She was the star of my life and the relationship we shared was deep and rich. She was the grandmother whom I wanted to live forever.

♥   ♥   ♥

In the spring of 1994, I got a job as a law clerk, working in Washington for a federal agency. I was assigned to a task force on a class action sexual discrimination suit. With my career moving upward and my marriage on solid ground, I was once again free to work in my church. God sent me a vision for a ministry which I named the Christian Adult Posse or CAP.

This ministry was designed to equip new adults, whom I classified as persons between the ages of seventeen and twenty-two, to be spiritually mature and grounded young adults. It provided them with the necessary tools to handle new freedoms and to conquer the temptations and pitfalls of young adult life. I was inspired with the ministry because I remembered the hell of my adolescence and young adult years, and I wanted to help make them easier for somebody else.

For young people, peer pressure can be a deadly process. Charting a path in life that is not filled with stress and turmoil requires work. I learned from my experiences how to fight physically, emotionally, and spiritually. I wanted to share my knowledge to help young people avoid my mistakes. I wanted to help young people avoid the "I'm grown up" syndrome and the mistakes that could lead to death. Although I had decided not to have children, I knew God wanted me to help children.

The CAP ministry gathered every Saturday afternoon at our church. It was a small group of young adults and three adult leaders, including myself. The young adults would share their challenges openly and honestly with the adults. We had an agreement that everything we shared was confidential. The young adults learned to trust us, and there was no subject that could not be discussed. Our meetings would last for two or more hours. Soon the young people started bringing their friends who were not members of the church. It was wonderful listening to their concerns as they talked about the temptations of young adulthood, such as sex and drugs, and about education and religion. It was phenomenal.

We began to love one another like a family who loves unconditionally and continually. The love that was generated in this ministry took root in my heart and it began to help me cope with Mama's condition.

On December 13, 1994, hallelujah, I was admitted to practice law in Maryland. I was rapturous. Finally I was an attorney. Goal achieved! I was so grateful and excited.

What happened next caught me by surprise. David began to feel threatened. The signs were subtle — maybe an expression on his face when I talked about how excited I was about my impending career. Subtle but, nonetheless, present.

I attempted to let him know that I was not going to change upon reaching a new plateau. Although how could I not change? I was now the person I prayed I would someday be, a well educated black woman. I was now the person whom I thought I would never see. How could I not change?

I wanted David to have confidence in me — confidence that everything would be all right, that I would not get big headed with my accomplishments, and that I would not leave him out of my life by putting my career before him.

In June 1995, just six months after admission to the bar, I started my own law practice. I shared office space with a classmate and best friend from law school. I had never anticipated opening my own law firm. As a legal secretary, I had worked for one of the most prestigious law firms in the country, and I knew that the operation of a law firm was not easy, but I was willing to try. I felt confident that because I knew what I did not want to do in my profession, such as criminal prosecution or defense, and that I could succeed doing something I knew I could do. I could help people to navigate their disappointment in love.

So I started a family-law practice, helping people with divorces, custody, visitation, and child support. If there was anything I knew about, it was certainly family and relationships. Initially things were slow. David was very supportive, maintaining the financial load when I had little or nothing to contribute.

I felt convinced that my family-law practice would succeed. I already knew about divorce, so it seemed to be a natural path. I also had a sincere desire to help people cope with their divorce. I knew firsthand the pain and disappointment associated with the process. I was now equipped to merge my personal and professional life. My pastor, as usual, was supportive and made an announcement in church. Little by little the clients came. After I completed a few divorces and custody cases, word spread quickly.

I used Mama's example as a base for dealing with people. I gave them respect and compassion, no matter what my opinion of their circumstances. I was sympathetic when I observed my clients crying, as they often did, because I knew firsthand their pain.

My life was starting to level off and at last I would have a sound marriage and a satisfying career. But everything was not wonderful.

Things with Mama got worse. The solid two-hundred-pound woman now weighed just a little under one hundred pounds. It was so painful watching her waste away. God was preparing her to die, this woman who was once healthy, strong, and vibrant, and I didn't want to watch her slow death anymore.

Again, I had to trust that God was working everything out for His purpose and for a good reason, but I was not enjoying this part of the journey. For months I cried and cried because I knew my relationship with Mama, as I had known it for thirty-five years, was now gone forever. I recalled the poem I wrote for Grandpa Zollie, "Nothing Remains the Same Forever," and it was surreal!

I tried to focus on all the good things in my life: a secure marriage, a blossoming career, and spiritual soundness. I was handling the goodness of my marriage and the sorrow of Mama's deteriorating health like a champ, but I was totally unprepared for what happened next.

In August 1995 some of the CAP members began to experience personal difficulties. Many times I couldn't do anything but pray, and I knew that worked.

The ministry had two presidents, one male and one female. First the male president was shot in the back while sitting in the backseat of a car. Thank God he lived and still lives today with the bullet in the muscles of his back. But what happened to Shanta, our female president of the ministry, is something out of a horror movie.

It was Saturday, September 9, 1995.

Shanta and I had developed a very close relationship. She was someone I considered as a little sister. We spent every Saturday together in the CAP ministry. My little sister began to confide in me her deepest secrets. Our bond was tight.

Shanta was a beautiful young woman in the prime of her life. Her skin was a silky, smooth milk-chocolate color. She had a tall, graceful frame, gorgeous brown eyes, and long flowing black hair. She was intelligent, charismatic, and her elegance could electrify a room. Her big radiant smile could light up the world. I expected the two of us to travel through life together for many years, sharing good times and fighting through the natural struggles.

That fatal Saturday I went to church, as usual, for the CAP meeting. Following our meeting I would always drive Shanta home. On this particular Saturday, when we arrived at her home, she did not get out the car right away. Instead, she asked if she could talk with me and, of course, I said yes.

I can still see her sitting in the passenger seat of my car, wearing a white Mickey Mouse T-shirt and jean shorts.

Shanta spoke in a soft quiet voice and she said to me, "I know you're going to be disappointed, but I'm pregnant."

After her confession, we talked for more than two hours, about her future because she was pregnant by a young man who was married. I was not livid with her but at the situation. Over a year ago I had begged her to get out of the relationship, but she didn't listen to me. I knew it spelled d-a-n-g-e-r! My heart sank as I listened to her confess her pain, confusion, doubts, fears, and dreams. As I listened, I prayed. I asked God to help me say the right thing. Despite my disappointment with Shanta, I had only one choice, so with my sincerest heart, I told her, "I will stand by you — no matter what." As our conversation ended, I vividly remember patting her on the leg and telling her, "Don't worry. You have your whole life ahead of you. I am disappointed, but we will get through this together."

At the time, little did I know my words were so far from the truth, I could not have imagined what would happen next.

We hugged each other and parted with the words, "I love you."

The next day was Sunday. David and I went to church. Around two that afternoon, David and I were relaxing at home. The telephone rang. David answered the phone, I heard him speaking softly, only saying, "Okay, okay." I wondered whom he was talking to, then he handed me the phone receiver.

I was immediately told that Shanta had been shot and killed. I fell to the floor.

Within less than twenty-four hours, after I told her she had her whole life ahead of her, she was dead. Shanta had been found dead in an alley, with four bullets to her abdomen and one bullet to her head.

Who would do such a horrible thing to such a beautiful young lady?

The police investigation began to unfold quickly, and I soon learned more details about Shanta's last hours of life. Apparently late during Saturday night and early in the morning hours of Sunday, Shanta left her safe home to meet the father of her unborn child, Curtis.

Within less than twenty minutes after she left home, a 911 call was received about a young woman screaming for help. Shanta was shot and left in an alley to die. It was clear to me that Curtis had killed her, and he obviously knew that he was going to kill her when he picked her up.

For me, it was starting again. Another murder, but this time it wasn't the perpetrator whom I loved, it was the victim.

The pain of losing Shanta was extreme — I wasn't sure I could handle it. After surviving the death of Daddy, I thought I could handle anything, but I was wrong. My grief consumed me. I struggled, trying to understand why Shanta had to die, and in such a horrific manner. I was angry with God. Yes, I was angry with God. My godmother told me after Daddy's death that God could handle Himself, that He was not afraid of me, so I could take all my feelings to Him. So I told God I was angry.

Shanta was young and naive in so many ways but she certainly didn't deserve to die the way she did. I was confounded.

I have a reverent fear for God, and my anger with Him was only momentary. I was angry because I was hurt, disappointed, and confused. I could not understand why he had to kill her. If he did not want to be a father to the child he did not have to, but to kill her to avoid fatherhood was something I could not comprehend.

David was the perfect husband during this ordeal. With his whole heart he consoled and supported me. There were many days and nights when I was like a helpless baby, and he held me in his arms while I cried.

Now it was the second time I would be confronted with a murder trial. I began to relive 1981 all over again: a married woman, a mistress, a pregnancy, and a murder.

Why was God allowing me to relive this pain? I could not understand why I had to endure two murder trials, one trial where the murderer was my loved one and one trial where the victim is my loved one. What I found was that I had compassion and understanding for both sides. I knew that the murderer didn't have to always be a mean, violent person without a conscience. The murderer can come from a family where there was love and structure. I knew that the victim, no matter what the circumstances, never deserved to be killed. I learned that everybody involved experiences pain.

Shanta was dead, and just as I knew instinctively who the killer was in Adam's case, I trusted that the evidence would prove me right in Shanta's case because I knew that Curtis killed Shanta from the moment I learned of her death.

Shanta told me Curtis's wife had learned of their relationship and she was freaking out about it. Shanta was over her head in this relationship. I fought with my emotions day and night and I prayed for justice.

Shortly after Shanta's funeral Curtis was arrested and charged with first-degree murder. This was just the beginning and it was still a long way to a conviction. I remembered it was a year before Adam went to trial, and that was fifteen years earlier when there were fewer murders.

As a child I had always heard that death came in threes. It happened that way in 1988: first Daddy, then Solomon's grandmother, then Uncle Joe.

Mama's condition had not changed. I was just standing on the sidelines waiting for her to die.

On November 8, 1995, Mama died. It was just two months after Shanta's murder. Strangely enough I was relieved that Mama had been set free from her distress and affliction. Before her strokes she had been a woman who was always happy, always finding ways to help others. The last two years of her life were spent in a wheelchair, unable to utter a word to the people she loved and cared about most. It killed her. The centerpiece of our family died, but I thought, at last, she was free.

I see Mama in the stars at night and in the sunshine in the morning. I watch the sky looking for her and Daddy.

The year 1995 had a grand finale. On a Friday evening in December, David and I had our regularly scheduled date, dinner at one of our favorite seafood restaurants. Unfortunately, the evening ended early because we had what I thought was a small argument.

The argument started when I asked David, "If I died, would you get married again?"

I was just making conversation. I thought, however, his reply was harsh and sarcastic. David said, with a tone of displeasure, "I will never get married again."

I interpreted the comment as a personal attack, and the evening ended abruptly.

We made up during the night and the next morning he went to work. I believed everything was fine.

That Saturday was a beautiful day. I went looking at houses. David and I had just begun our search for our first home. We had been married for over four years, and I knew we had made it through the worst period and our marriage was secure.

When David came home from work, he was in an unusual mood. He was not upbeat and he made little eye contact with me.

I was excited to tell him about the house search although my heart was still aching with grief over the death of Mama and Shanta. In some respects, I was in denial about Mama's death. I would not talk about Mama and I tried my best not to think of her. I did that because it was too painful! On the other hand, I thought of Shanta and her killer regularly. It would have been great to fade away into denial about her death too, but it was impossible with the impending trial.

When David walked into the house, I ran up to him and joyfully began to share my excitement about the houses. David softly said to me, "Sit down, I need to tell you something."

Not saying a word, I sat down on the sofa. David said, "I want to separate."

Chapter 4

Radical Obedience!

David and I had been married for four and a half years. We lived together harmoniously. I am not saying it was perfect, but it was fulfilling, joyful, and peaceful.

Now he wanted to separate. I was shocked! When he told me, I just sat there on the couch, trying to figure out if I had just heard what I thought I heard.

I didn't know what to do, but calmness came over me. It was strange. I did not want to argue and I did not want to talk.

I looked at David and softly said, "Okay."

Just prior to David coming home, I was listening to one of my favorite gospel artists, Hezekiah Walker. He had just released a new CD entitled *By Any Means Necessary.* So just before David walked in, I was in a good place listening to music. So when I heard David say those shocking words to me, that he wanted to separate, I was calm. I attributed my calmness to the inspirational lyrics and melodious tones of the music. Even full of shock, I had the fortitude to go back to my music and begin to seek God.

I could have died, but somehow I managed to hear the voice of Jesus whisper "be calm" and I did just that. I stayed calm although it seemed impossible. I knew God told me to be still so I waited to hear from Him before I made any decisions. In the past I reacted to my emotions and immediately began to make decisions which, in retrospect, were not always good choices.

David told me that he wanted us to separate because he needed some space because he had gotten married too fast. I thought, this is unreal, he is crazy, or maybe I am! There had to be more to it. I knew that David was stressed with working two jobs, stressed with his children's mothers constantly criticizing him and needing more money, stressed with not having enough money. With all the stresses that life can bring, I thought David and I were handling them well.

Now another separation was looming over my head. Many days I tried to act like everything was fine — I went to work and to church — but some things I could not hide. I confided in my friends, and they were in disbelief. One or two became very angry; I knew it was because they were hurt too.

David did not leave right away, but he was making plans to leave.

The new year came and it was not a happy occasion. I was devastated by my impending separation from David. This would be the third time I would be going down this road and I thought I was finished with this torture.

During this time David and I did not argue. We continued to be cordial and respectful to each other. He kept telling me that it was him and not me, that he needed some space because he was stressed out.

By the beginning of February David had found an apartment and started making preparations to move.

I just patiently waited to hear from God. I had no idea what to do. I wanted my marriage to last and I was trying my best not to lose my mind. I had come so far emotionally and spiritually and now I was facing another marital dilemma.

I recall one Wednesday, while attending Noon Day Service at church, I just fell apart. I cried and I cried. I felt like I was reliving a nightmare. I could not understand why my life was taking the same road over again, marriage, separation, death, and divorce.

I made it from day to day because God empowered me. Daily, I depended on the word of God to give me the strength and joy I needed to make it through.

I had to maintain my law practice. It was my only source of income and that meant helping other people when I was feeling sick inside, listening to my clients talk about their ensuing divorce, and trying not to drown in my own sorrow.

I thought David had lost his mind. We had a good marriage. We were both happy or, at least, I thought we were. He never said he wasn't happy. What did he need space to do?

I asked him to pray and make sure he knew that he was doing the right thing. He said he had prayed, and he was doing the right thing. I accepted his word, even though I didn't believe it.

Again my days became filled with the struggle to stay strong and to stay positive. I was confused in my spirit. I asked God, why? What was I going to do? I didn't want another divorce. I told God I would do anything. God told me again to stand still. It wasn't the answer I was looking for. I was willing to beg and plead to keep my marriage.

Now I had to wait for clarity and direction. It was not easy or enjoyable.

I was afraid for David. I knew that the pitfalls of life were trying to capture and destroy him, just the way it happened for Adam. I was afraid he would regret his decision and that it would be life-altering for both of us.

David moved out on February 14, 1996. Déjà vu — I was back in time, in 1981, when Adam also left me on February 14, the all-significant Valentine's Day.

I asked God, why, why, why? Why was I here again?

David gave me his address and his telephone number.

I was down but I couldn't let it show. I had to keep my law practice running because it was thriving. I began to practice some criminal defense work, directly related to all the drama of relationships: stalking, malicious destruction of property, assault, and domestic violence. For me every day was "drama city." In court, people were fighting over their children, not always considering the impact on them but many times acting out of selfishness and meanness. Every opportunity I got, I said something that Mama taught me, to help them stop hating and start loving more.

I wanted to help my clients to overcome their adversities. I encouraged them to go forward with their dreams and, if they didn't have a dream outside their now-fractured relationship, to create a dream and work on making it come true. That's what I was attempting to do in my own life and it was working.

I protected my clients as if they were my own children. I laughed with them, I cried with them, and I guided them through the legal process. It was important to me that they find victory in what could be a defeating moment.

I had no other choice but to keep myself together and stay strong, and I learned to function with my pain.

While working, I thought of David and the great marriage we had. He was my best friend, my husband, and now we were separated.

I remembered how we met and how the relationship progressed. We gave great thought to our decision to marry. We discussed our dreams and relayed our expectations. What went wrong?

I was still young, only thirty-five, but I felt as though I had been living a lifetime of marital discord. Nonetheless, with all the pain I was enduring, I used my early survival tactics to sustain me.

I believe the will to survive is an instinct. Surely, I did not know how to survive a divorce but, instinctively, I knew I had to survive. Because I had a desire to survive, I had to develop heartbreak and divorce survival skills.

I went back to writing in my journals. Throughout the years since 1983, I had sporadically kept a journal. I had learned that by writing my thoughts I was able to get in touch with my true emotions. I used my journal entries to help me reflect on what I should do to improve my state of mind. I now understood that my writings were a road map through my confusion.

I went back to dining out alone. I did it before and I could do it again. Now, some evenings, I would get dressed up just like I was going on a date. I would choose a restaurant suitable for my appetite and I had a meal alone and I enjoyed it. I had learned to enjoy being by myself. I still had my Friday night Chinese food and a Humphrey Bogart movie, Saturday at CAP meeting, and all day Sunday at church. I was still content, but I missed David. David had stopped attending our church, and I had few opportunities to see him.

I was determined that I was not going to let this separation kill me, destroy my joy, or cause me to regress into depression and confusion.

I was in a much better place now than I was ten years ago. I had intellectual and financial security. I had achieved my goal of becoming an attorney, I was on the road to success, and I was starting to love myself. I was content with so many aspects of my life, but why could I not get this marriage thing right? The separation between David and me only added new depth to my perplexity about marriage and how it works and why it sometimes dies.

I was still shocked that David and I were not together. Did he lie about why he wanted to separate?

Shortly after David moved out, it dropped into my spirit that there was more to David leaving than just that "he needed space." I didn't suspect him of infidelity because there had been no signs, unlike Adam who stayed out all night and whose paramour harassed both him and me. Nonetheless, I decided to check his answering machine. It was our machine and I still had the access code. I was only doing what people do when they are suspicious — start looking for evidence to corroborate suspicions.

Much to my disappointment I heard a message from a woman thanking David for a wonderful evening, detailing their intimate acts. I almost fainted. I was so disgusted with David. I should have been angry, but I wasn't angry, just disgusted. I thought, I should have known! Unfortunately, I did not recognize the voice. Who was this woman?

In the short time that I had been practicing family law I was seeing that infidelity was the number one reason behind marital strife, with money running to tie first place.

I was disgusted because in my opinion there was no reason for David's lying and infidelity except selfishness! I had done everything to make our marriage satisfying for both of us. Now his infidelity was staring me in the face.

Over the years David and I had worked hard to build a strong and trusting marriage. How could he? Not only did he hurt me, but he had also betrayed our network of family and friends who loved us both. I was numb and in disbelief.

I called David and I told him that I had checked his messages and heard the message from his lover. His only response was, "I'm sorry!" I told him that I was hurt and that he lied to me about why he wanted to separate. David continued to say, "I'm sorry." He said, "I promise you, I didn't lie, I didn't leave you for another woman." I actually believed David because I knew him to not be a liar; he was sometimes too honest. I also knew that David had trouble being celibate.

Although I was hurt and disappointed with David, I still loved him and we had a good life together and I recognized it. I kept working on my career and creating a successful law practice.

Phillip started attending my church. We had never stopped being friends. He would call me occasionally, but I had never allowed our friendship to interfere with my marriage. Now, I started fantasizing that after so many years as friends Phillip and I would get married and live happily ever after. Although I was still married and in love with David, the fantasy of being happily married to Phillip was a great way to escape the pain inside my broken heart. It's funny how distractions work. Sometimes they can be good. My fantasy of Phillip distracted me from thinking about how hurt I was that David had left me and was having an intimate relationship with another woman. I am not saying it was the right thing to do; I am just saying this is what I did. I know that coping is an individual activity and people cope differently. My rule is to cope in a way so that you do not hurt yourself or anyone else.

One day after Noon Day Service, Phillip asked me to lunch. Although I had not spoken to him about my recent separation, he knew something was wrong because David had not been to church with me and I sat alone, usually crying.

I met Phillip at a restaurant downtown. We greeted with a hug. After we were seated he immediately said, "What did David do?" I expected us to engage in some small talk before getting to the point. I told him, "He left."

He said, "Some other woman."

I said, "Yes."

As I began to cry he said to me, "Look, you are a smart woman. You are a lawyer. You are a pretty woman and you can make it without a man and you know you can get a man, you got me."

Would my fantasy that Phillip would ask me to marry him come true? He was forty-six, had never been married, and always had at least two women. I was fantasizing about being married to this man who had never had a monogamous relationship. The fantasy was truly only a fantasy because I did not trust Phillip and I had little confidence that he would ever change. What I really wanted was for David and me to work out our problems and live happily married.

About a month after discovering that David had been sleeping with another woman, the lease at our apartment expired and I moved back to my apartment in Ellicott City among the oak trees.

It was not until April, after I had time to calm down, when I began to hear the voice of God.

One afternoon David came to my office. That was not strange because we had maintained our communication, even though we were not together. Even in light of my discovery of his infidelity, we continued to have regular conversations. It was normal for David and me to talk because we were friends and we had good communication.

But on this day, I never expected David to say, "I want to come home."

It was just what I wanted to hear, right?

Wrong!

With a calm and steady voice, I said to him, "I am not ready for that yet."

What? I thought to myself, are you crazy? This was my husband, the man I loved truly and deeply, and now he wanted to return home. What was I not ready for? We were married. Was I being selfish now?

No. I was being protective.

I knew I was too afraid to trust him again with my heart. My heart was already broken into many pieces. There was the hurt from Adam, the hurt from Solomon, the hurt of my loved ones dying, Grandpa Zollie, Daddy, Uncle Joe, Mama, and Shanta. I knew my heart was fragile and I knew I had to protect it.

I had to protect me. I had to protect my mental and emotional well-being. I was not going to let David take me on an emotional roller coaster ride. How could I trust him to stay if he came back? How could I trust him not to see her again? How could I trust him to be honest?

I was confounded with making the right choice for the moment, and the right choice for my future. I had no idea where I was headed with my personal life.

At thirty-five I had a whole different outlook on life from when I was twenty-one, when Adam and I separated, and from when I was twenty-four, when Solomon and I separated. I had matured some, and I had gained some emotional strength and mental power. I learned to love myself. I had learned to consider the risks associated with my decisions and actions. I was different.

When I told David I was not ready to reconcile, he looked disappointed, but I stayed my course because I had some understanding.

When David told me he wanted to separate, I didn't understand why God told me to be calm, but now it made sense. I had to be calm because there was more ahead. I had to be calm because I had to function in my law practice. I had to be calm so that I could hear His voice clearly. I had searched for some understanding, now I had it, and I wanted to keep moving in the right direction.

I thank God for an intimate understanding of His word and a deep belief in His power. At this juncture I had learned to trust my spirit, that inner voice that we all possess. It kept saying to me, "Everything is going to be just fine." I recited the scripture, "And we know that in all things God works for the good of those who love Him, who have been called according to His purpose." I did not understand what was happening, but I believed it was going to work out for my good.

On April 6, 1996, Papa died. Mama had been dead only seven months. The funeral was surreal. Ms. Alberta, her family and our family, we were all together. Papa and Mama had been separated for forty years. They never divorced, even after Papa had a son with Ms. Alberta and Mr. Kelly started living with Mama. They were buried beside each other. It seemed strange to me, but clearly everybody had accepted the circumstances. Mr. Kelly had accepted that Papa was Mama's legal husband and he still loved her. Ms. Alberta accepted that Mama was Papa's legal wife and she loved him. Crazy it may seem, but love can make people do crazy things. I am just thankful that everybody managed their feelings so that there was never any conflict.

Just a few weeks later, and two months after David and I separated, I attended a two-day retreat with some of my sisters in Christ. The retreat was sponsored by one of my best friends. I fondly call her JoJo.

David and I were very close with JoJo and her husband. JoJo was devastated that David and I were separated, to say the least. She loved us together and she wanted me to make it through what she knew was a very difficult time for me.

The retreat was held in Pennsylvania at Camp Agape, nestled on 250 acres with sprawling mountains, a majestic sight. I could see the grandness of nature and the exhibition of God's work on full display. I was ecstatic. Over the years nature had become one of my best balancers: the sunrise, my rocks, the sky, the stars and the moon; they were my grounding. Whatever the circumstance, I learned to look up and in the sky I always found peace and encouragement. I was just where I needed to be, close to nature.

When I arrived at the mountains, I knew I needed direction. I knew I needed to hear from God. I was looking to find an explanation why I was divorced twice and now separated.

I got just what I needed!

There I was at Camp Agape, surrounded by the magnificent beauty of God's creation. I turned my focus from David and me and I started focusing on myself.

The retreat was phenomenal. Its purpose was for women to explore being female and how we think and react as women. We were a group of about twenty.

After a brief introduction from every woman, a bag was passed around with our names in it. Each woman had to select a name without disclosing it. You could identify the woman only as your "secret prayer partner." The object was for each woman to pray every day for her secret partner without revealing her identity. Having a secret prayer partner meant that everyone prayed for someone else without knowing her needs or concerns. The object was to develop a stronger prayer life by trusting your intuition to pray for others.

The retreat was eye-opening. Our session leaders were mature women who were wise and knowledgeable about the pitfalls and victories in life. We freely and openly discussed being female and all the dynamics of being a woman.

One particular session, taught by the Reverend Adella Hope, was so surreal for me. Growing up, I wanted a lot of siblings, which never happened. But God obviously heard my prayer because He sent me a lot of true friends, women and men whom I trust and rely on, whom I love and they love me. My treasure of friends, my brothers and sisters, stood by me and supported me, at times when I wanted to give up.

So on this day, Rev. Hope said, "Every woman needs at least seven women in her life." I was astounded because I had more than seven women in my life. She described how each woman played a different role: a "comforter" who provides hugs and healing, a "clarifier" who will help us see things clearly, a "confronter" who will help us face our issues, a "collaborator" who helps us compose our goals, a "companion" we share our time with, a "confidant" whom you can to talk to about anything without fear of chastisement or judgment, and a "colleague" who understands our work!

As she spoke, I was able to identify a woman in my life who fulfilled every role described. I felt that my life was in order in this respect and I knew I was fortunate.

On the last morning of the retreat a few of the woman gathered to climb the scenic mountain. Before we embarked on our journey, one of the leaders asked each of us to write a prayer on a piece of paper, to write down one thing we wanted to receive from God.

I pondered my heart and asked myself the question, "What is the one thing I want from God?"

After a few minutes, following her instructions, I wrote on a small yellow piece of paper the following words: *Lord Jesus, I want to be more obedient.* At the time I didn't really understand why I even wrote those words — a prayer for obedience? I didn't think I had been disobedient, but I wrote what I heard in my spirit.

I asked myself, "How have I been disobedient?" My mother had taught me as a child to be obedient. To me that included no lying, no stealing, and all the other commandments of the Bible. When I was a child the consequence of my disobedience was punishment.

As an adult I thought that if I lived by simplistic Godly principles, by abstaining from social and immoral wrongs, I was being obedient. Was I mistaken?

I carried my prayer for obedience in my pocket to the top of the mountain. From the top was a regal view. I stood on a platform high above the ground. I saw God's radiance across the trees. I felt His power as I focused on a sign directly in front of me which read "Jesus."

On this day my life was forever changed.

On the mountain I prayed, I worshiped, I cried, and I spent time talking with God.

I felt so good after returning from the mountain, although I still had no understanding of why my life had been so very different from what I imagined and expected. I was feeling empowered but I was still waiting to hear from God about my prayer for obedience.

During the same evening all the women gathered for our closing exercise in a large room. At last, the time had come for us to reveal the identity of our secret prayer partner.

Each lady gave a description of her secret prayer partner and then would say, "And this woman is . . ." and announce her name.

As I sat there listening to each description, I waited for my name to be announced. After a few women had been identified a woman seated across the room from me stood up. I did not know her. She introduced herself and began by describing this woman she had observed in her church, a woman she had admired from afar. She talked about watching this woman and the way she conducted herself at church. She said that this woman inspired her, and she was fascinated with the way the woman praised God.

At the conclusion of her very gracious remarks, she said, "This woman is Avalon."

I was stunned! I had listened to a stranger — a woman who attended the same church with me and I had never noticed her. Yet, she had noticed me and had made some positive judgments about me. Mama used to say to me, "You never know who is watching so always put your best foot forward." This lady had watched me and, unbeknownst to me, I had the opportunity to make either a positive or negative impression on her. I am thankful I was able to make a positive impression. It is the way I have tried to live my life, adhering to the wise advice of my grandmother.

I was in awe that my secret prayer partner, now known as Janice, described a strong woman of good character whom she admired, who I never guessed was me. But that didn't startle me as much as what happened next.

She then handed me a small paperback book and said, "God told me to give you this book." When I looked at the title, I almost passed out: *The Life of Obedience* by Kenneth Hagin, Jr. I knew at that very moment that God was speaking to me.

My life has not been the same since I received that divinely inspired and written message. The experience and the book changed my entire life.

I was grateful to my secret prayer partner for being a tool that helped to transform my life. I hoped to see her again at church.

After returning from the retreat, I did not start reading my book immediately. I got involved again with my life, my law practice, church, singing in the choir, ushering, and the CAP ministry. With all that to keep me busy, the fact remained that David and I were still separated.

Life seemed to be moving along. I felt energized from the retreat. I was still pondering my question to God that I asked on the mountaintop. It was nagging at my spirit. I kept wondering and asking myself the same question, "How was I disobedient?" I was a responsible adult, independent, honest, and kind.

Why did I need to ask God to help me be more obedient?

David and I were separately struggling with our identity. I knew he missed me because whenever we spoke he said, "I miss you, Avalon." He wanted us to reconcile but he had made a grave mistake by having the affair with the woman I now knew as Melanie. David knew of my past heartaches and he knew I was not going to just accept his infidelity without considering the impact on me.

I must admit that I did miss David too, but I was scared to trust him with my love again. I was bruised from all the hurt. I had diligently tried to make our marriage work. David had abruptly ended our marriage with just a few words: "I need some space so I want to separate." Those words cut me like a knife. Then I found out he was having an affair with Melanie. My wounds were still healing. I knew if we were to get back together, it was going to take a lot of hard work. We would both have to overcome our emotions of regret, betrayal, disappointment, and hurt.

I was glad that since our separation, David and I had continued to have intermittent conversations. This allowed us to work on healing, by affirming our love for one another and our sorrow for the mistakes. I was disappointed that David had gotten involved with Melanie. I had begun to hear rumors that David had been seeing her before we separated. People were now telling me about when they saw them out together, and it only exacerbated my festering emotions of hurt and disgust. However, my pain did not erase the love that I had for David and I still desired to have him in my life. I wasn't sure if I would remain his wife but I knew our love still existed. No matter what David did I still loved him. I have accepted that love can be like a coin, and it has two sides. One side is filled with love and satisfaction and the other side is filled with hurt and disappointment.

I asked God, "Why did David leave me?" Was it because he needed more space? Was it because he was involved with Melanie? I had to do some more deep soul searching. This time I didn't go searching for evidence; I just waited to hear from God, to hear that voice that lives deep inside of me, the same voice that encouraged me to follow my dream of becoming an attorney. Now, I waited again for more spiritual guidance.

On a Sunday afternoon, David called and asked me if I could come over to his apartment. This was strange because in the seven months that we had been separated, he had never invited me to his apartment. I heard the urgency in his voice, and he said that it was very important.

I went directly to David's apartment. When I arrived there, I got sick because when we separated we agreed that he would take the living-room furniture and now it was staring me in the face. It looked so much like what used to be our home. A thousand memories flooded my mind about the years we spent together, dancing and singing to our music, long romantic nights with passionate lovemaking, family gatherings with laughter filling the room. Suddenly I was consumed by the grief of reality.

I sat down on the couch. David sat across from me. He began, "How have you been?"

I told him I was fine, although I was not totally fine, but I was coping with the disappointments of my life.

David said to me, "I have something that I need to tell you, and I am sorry. I did not want you to hear this from anyone else."

I began thinking, "Oh no, does he have some fatal disease? Is he going to die?"

Nothing could have ever prepared me for what he said.

"Melanie is pregnant."

I was shocked, but maybe I shouldn't been. Melanie was the woman who put the vulgar messages, which she thought was sexy, on my husband's answering machine. She was the woman who was gallivanting around town with my husband.

I wanted to die and I could have killed her and David. My head felt like it was going to explode.

My pager went off. I looked at the number. It was Phillip. I had seen him that morning in church. Since that lunch in March, we had continued to spend time together, going to dinner and shopping. Our dates were usually spontaneous, when Phillip was available.

I immediately told David, "I have to leave." It felt like the room was spinning.

David stood there, looking at me and repeating, "I am so sorry."

I left, and I thought to myself, what the hell is going on? How could Melanie be pregnant? How could David let that happen? What was I going to do now? I had too much going on to lose my mind. I had to maintain my new law practice and to be emotionally prepared for the upcoming trial of Shanta's killer.

It was late August and, after almost a year, Curtis was brought to trial for killing Shanta.

Another murder trial, but this time, I was seeing things from a different perspective. With Adam, the focus was his defense; with Shanta, the focus was the prosecution of the perpetrator. It was an arduous and traumatic task. I provided whatever assistance I could to the prosecutor because I was with Shanta the evening she was killed. I knew the elaborate details of her intentions to tell Curtis of her pregnancy. The prosecutor was God-sent, a man of God, who prayed with us and for us. He was brilliant in all aspects of the case and he never gave up in our fight for justice. Curtis was convicted of first-degree murder and sentenced to life in prison, without the possibility of parole.

♥ ♥ ♥

David and I had been separated for eight months.

Melanie was now six months pregnant and the baby was expected in late January 1997.

Since our separation, David and I had not been together intimately. We had continued to talk on the phone and we had seen each other a few times. I was surely not going back that way now, but I still loved him and I was desperately missing our marriage and so was David.

Every year, the last week in November, my church has a revival. I usually attended but, much to my amazement, David also showed up.

I was shocked but I was overjoyed to see him in church. Our friends greeted him with warm hugs and big smiles. After the service, he came over to me. He was crying. He asked if he could see me and I said yes.

I left church and met David at his apartment. We talked and we talked and we talked all night. He apologized over and over again. He told me that he did not leave me for Melanie, that he met her when he remodeled her kitchen. At that time, she was also married. He thought it was only a fling and then she got pregnant. He poured his heart out to me and I felt his regret and sincerity. He said he missed me and he asked me to reconcile with him.

I didn't know what to do.

I talked with my pastor and, with prompting from him and our friends, we reconciled.

I accepted the reality that Melanie was going to have David's baby and tried my best to live with it and move on.

Our friends were very supportive. They loved David and me together. Our breakup had been traumatic for many of them; now they saw David as a man who loved me, who made a mistake, who was sorry for his mistake, and was now ready to go forward with our marriage. They too were willing to forgive him.

I made one fatal mistake: I never asked God if it was the right thing to do because I knew it had to be — we were married.

I moved some of my clothes into David's apartment and left my furniture in my apartment. I had a one-year lease and I was not going to break it and jeopardize my credit, so I kept my apartment.

I must admit it was a big adjustment moving into David's apartment, but I tried to cope with the change.

I searched for contentment. I was not comfortable internally being with David. I could not understand why: he was my husband, I loved him deeply, I knew he loved me, but something just was not right.

Throughout the holiday season David and I were together.

The new year arrived: 1997. Unfortunately, I was more uncomfortable now than ever. I struggled to forget the discomfort I was feeling in my spirit.

God took me back to my obedience book. I had started reading the book, but I wasn't finished yet. The book had only twenty-eight pages and I was taking more than a year to complete it because, after I read the first chapter, God dealt with me for almost six months, as I wrestled to try to comprehend how I had been disobedient. The first chapter concentrates on the Biblical story of the disobedience of King Solomon, and how his disobedience cost him his throne and life.

While reading, digesting, and meditating on this word, I remember God speaking to me and saying, "I am going to tell you to do something just like I told King Solomon." God said, "Nobody is going to understand why you are doing it, but do it." I didn't pay much attention to the directive. At first I was too busy dealing with my consciousness of my disobedience.

Through this small book on obedience, I was forced to take a look at my choices in life. I had to think about my choice to marry David knowing that he was ambivalent and that I was hesitant to try marriage a third time. I had to ponder my choice to accept his infidelity. I had to ponder how my choice to reconcile would impact me since David would now have a new baby with Melanie, a woman I did not care to have any contact with.

It was the middle of January and Melanie's baby was due soon. I was tormented by the thought of my being David's wife and her being his former mistress with his baby. Yet I considered my vow to stand by David through the good and the bad. What I didn't know was if I could handle the stress of the bad: the late-night calls from Melanie about the baby and the strain of knowing that this woman was going to be a part of my life. It had not happened yet, but it was only a matter of time before all the drama would begin. I was starting a new career which I had worked hard to accomplish and, even without Melanie and the baby, that created its own stress. I was a little older and a little wiser and I had learned that I had limitations. I had discovered through my years of tears with Adam and Solomon that my emotions run deep and if I did not manage the stress of coping with my deep emotions, my emotions could cripple and eventually kill me. I knew that this would be an emotional roller coaster ride for me. I knew myself well enough to know that I would always feel the pain of David's betrayal every time Melanie's name was mentioned, and her name would be mentioned for years to come as she reached out to get support for her child from David. For me that meant there would always be thoughts of David's adultery. I wondered what God wanted me to do because I wanted to be a good wife and I loved David.

I asked God to help me. He said what I never expected Him to say. He said, "Leave."

I thought I heard wrong so I ignored it, but deep inside I knew I heard the voice of God speaking to me, clearly and correctly. I felt it way down in my spirit and I cried out to God to help me understand. I wanted the marriage to work. Why did I have to leave?

God did not answer right away.

With each passing day David and I were getting deeper into our relationship. At the same time I was more and more uncomfortable living with him. I kept thinking of what I would do when Melanie called and said, it's time, the baby is coming.

Since my experience on the mountaintop with God, He had slowly and delicately taken me through my life of marriage and my choice to divorce. I had made some good and bad choices. I had not consulted God for every decision and some of my choices took me down a road of pain and despair. This time I wanted to make the right choice for my life and that meant listening to God. I believe in purpose and where there is purpose there is direction. I was seeking the right direction for my life. I did not want to be disobedient to the will of God for my life. I learned that in the past I had been disobedient.

How was I disobedient? I married in love, I married in the church, and I married with every intention of being married only once until death do us part.

How had I been disobedient?

Maybe I was too impatient. Maybe I should have waited to get married the first time. Maybe I should not have divorced Adam. Maybe I should not have married Solomon. Maybe I should not have divorced Solomon. Maybe I should not have married David. Maybe I was impulsive.

Did I make my own plans based on what I thought was best for me and ignore God's plans for my life?

I had often thought that maybe I should have waited for Adam to get out of jail. I loved him enough to wait. I still love him. He is still in jail and where would I be now, if I had waited?

My second marriage had clear signs of caution. From the beginning I asked God to guide me. I felt I was making a mistake, my family told me I was making a mistake. There I was, the church filled with family and friends, two days after Christmas and Solomon's birthday. Should I have walked out? Should I have embarrassed my family? Should I have left Solomon at the altar? Should I have disappointed his family?

I could see where there could have been disobedience in my marriages to Adam and Solomon, but it was not clear to me where the disobedience lay with David and me.

Our marriage was very different from my first two. David and I were both over thirty when we married, supposedly more mature. We were both in Christ. We both understood the seriousness of our vows. We were willing to do what was necessary to make our marriage work.

Maybe we should have waited. Maybe we never should have separated. Maybe we should not have reconciled.

The questions of life — and I had to find a satisfactory answer to them all. I wanted to live free of these problems, never to repeat them again.

I continued reading the chapters in my obedience book, praying for clarity and guidance. I could not sleep at night. I kept crying out to God for a clear answer about David and me. Finally, He answered me.

I knew then that I had to leave David. We had reconciled and were committed to trying to make it work, but I had to end it. I knew after my first night there I had to leave, but it took me almost two months to act. Every time I thought I should get out, something seemed to happen to pull me in. This time I had to be obedient.

I began a new chapter in my obedience book titled "The Consequences of Being Disobedient." I heard God talking so loudly, I was in a panic until I got out. I fought against myself and my friends. I fought against David and I decided I was going to leave.

It was January 17, 1997. Melanie was due to have her baby any day. The inside of my body felt like a washing machine constantly running on the spin cycle. I felt strongly in my spirit that I had to leave immediately.

The next day David and I talked about my leaving. He said he understood, but I knew he was crushed. David loved me even more now than ever. I said to David what was later proven to be prophetic: "This baby is not coming until after I am gone."

On January 20, 1997, David and I had spent the weekend together. I left for work from his apartment that Monday morning, and that evening I moved to my sanctuary in the valley of oak trees, my apartment encased in serenity.

For the first time in my adult life I felt that I was being obedient to God in my choices.

The next day, my first morning back in my apartment was stupendous. As I opened my eyes I beheld the majestic beauty of the rising of the sun, brightly shining in my face. I knew I was in the right place. I was energized.

The phone rang and it was David. His conversation started with generalities, then he said, "Melanie had the baby."

I immediately thought of the words from my spirit, this baby is not coming until after I am gone. I had been in my apartment only twenty-four hours. I was so thankful to God I listened to Him when He told me to leave. Now with the news of the baby's arrival, I was in an environment where I felt emotionally safe and strong. I was peaceful.

I asked David, "What is it, a boy or a girl?"

He said, "A boy."

I asked what hospital Melanie and the baby were in. David told me and I said to him, "I am coming to see the baby."

He said in disbelief, "You are going to do what?"

I told him again, "I am coming to see the baby."

"Are you sure you want to do that?"

I replied calmly, "Yes."

I showered and dressed. As I drove to the hospital I was perplexed. I didn't know why I was going to see this baby. I had never seen Melanie, and I had no interest in meeting her, yet I knew I had to go.

When I first arrived at the hospital I went into the gift shop. I purchased a card and a small stuffed animal. The front of the card read "May God Bless You and Your New Baby."

I got on the elevator and made my way to the maternity ward.

When the elevator doors opened David was standing there. We kissed and greeted each other. We walked down the hall and entered Melanie's room. David walked in first.

As we entered the room David said to me, "Avalon, this is Melanie." She was lying in the bed wearing a blue printed hospital gown. I had never given much thought to what Melanie looked like; it didn't matter to me. So when I first saw her all I could see was a woman who had committed adultery with my husband and had his baby. I had learned from Phillip that Melanie was also married, so I also felt sympathy for her husband. It's a small world and Phillip knew Melanie's husband and he spoke of his pain.

As I looked at Melanie lying in that bed holding David's child, I could almost hear David's heart beating from across the room. He was nervous but I was not. At last I was face to face with Melanie.

I said, "Hello," and handed her the card and gift.

She said, "Thank you."

David asked me if I wanted to sit down; I said, "Yes."

Except for the whisper of the television there was silence in the room.

Melanie asked me, "Would you like to hold the baby?"

I said, "No thank you."

Again, silence filled the room. After about two minutes, I said to Melanie, "Take care." I told David, "I am leaving."

David said, "I will walk you to the elevator."

We left the room together and walked in silence to the elevator. Before the elevator arrived David said to me, "Why did you do this to yourself? Are you okay?"

I replied, "Yes."

The elevator came, we kissed, and I got on it.

David said, "I'll call you later."

I said, "Okay."

No matter how uncomfortable the situation, David and I could talk about anything. I knew we had to talk about my feelings and his feelings. This was one of the most awkward situations I ever faced in my life and maybe for him too.

I went home to my apartment, my place of refuge, and I began to ponder if David and I could ever reconcile.

My thoughts focused on the precious little boy who was innocent. I knew this child needed his father. Every child should be blessed to have a good father. I recalled my own joyful childhood and the great relationship that I had with my father. I wanted this child to know the same joy I knew.

But I knew it would not happen with me in the picture, not at this time, because I wanted absolutely nothing to do with Melanie. But I couldn't separate her from her baby. I knew that I was unwilling to have Melanie in my life and if David and I reconciled, she would be a part of our life. She would be calling for money, calling for diapers, calling for milk. She would want David to come over and see the baby. She would want to bring the baby to him. It would have been one interaction after another for at least eighteen years. She would tug and pull at David until I was in a frenzy. I knew it would be a nightmare for me and I wanted only the best for the baby boy.

As the next months passed, I saw less of David. Our conversations were few and far between. I spent time with myself, building my law practice, staying committed to my spiritual growth.

I began to put my obedience into practice. I began learning how to listen to God more attentively.

During the summer of 1997 I was transitioning from my prior life of disobedience, when I did whatever I thought would make me happy and in love.

I was transitioning to being content single, and waiting for direction from God before making a decision about love and marriage. I was unsure if I would ever be in love deeply again.

On July 26, 1997, I penned a poem. As I read it today, I understand how unclear I was about what I should do with my love.

What should I do with Love?

How shall I handle it?

Should I caress it and hold it?

Should I secure it and lock it up?

Should I kill it so that it never spreads?

What should I do with Love?

Is it tender and sweet?

It is soft and wet, cold and dry?

What should I do with Love?

I don't know and you probably don't either,

So we will journey together. Climb the mountains,

Soar the sky and maybe, just maybe

We will recognize Love when we get there.

I knew I would never stop loving David. I filed for divorce.

Chapter 5

Embracing Reality!

August 17, 1997, was my thirty-seventh birthday. I celebrated in one of my usual fashions and went to the Atlantic Ocean to see the sunrise. For many years now, I had used the sunrise as a mechanism for me to gain clarity in my life. I felt strength as I watched the sun come over the horizon. I discovered comfort in the ocean and inspiration in the serenity of watching God bring the sun over the horizon and illuminate the earth. After watching many sunrises, I have concluded no two are the same. Each year I experience something new and awakening. It was the perfect setting for me to reflect on my life and my circumstances: once again, separated and waiting for the divorce to be final.

It was this year that I began the tradition of celebrating my birthday for the entire month of August. I discovered that one day was just not enough for me to do all the things I love to do: a trip to the ocean, a trip to the mountains, a party, a party, and another party, friends, family, lots of good music, dancing, laughter, and genuine love. Love is the center of my existence, and I love to celebrate with the people I love!

Now I sat on the beach watching the sun come over the horizon, thanking God for my peace and rejoicing in my soundness of mind. I could have been depressed, but instead, I felt grateful that once again I had passed through the dark and often traumatizing doors of divorce and I survived with love still in my heart.

I was excited because my life was good. I was not the same woman who divorced Adam some fourteen years earlier. I was now a confident lady not ashamed that I was divorced three times. In Hollywood it is okay to be divorced multiple times, but in real life, it is taboo. It can be a lonely and painful road to travel, and I made it.

I was actually amazed that I had grown into such a confident lady because my self-esteem had been challenged so many times. First in junior high school, when a few girls were jealous of me and I struggled to understand why. I didn't think I was beautiful, so why were they jealous? Then in my marriages: first Adam and his infidelity and then David. I was shocked that I felt so good about being myself.

For over fifteen years I only imagined that someday I would be financially secure, emotionally grounded, spiritually rooted, intellectually sound, and just downright happy and satisfied, in spite of all my losses.

I watched the sun come over the horizon and I thanked God for every tear and every smile. I thanked Him for the good days and the hard and lonely nights, because finally I was grounded in my reality and I had overcome my disappointment of not being married and not being a wife.

Special occasions can be hard on single people and divorced persons. I taught myself to love my special events. Some women hate to celebrate their birthday, but not me.

Finally, I had accepted my fate as good, and I embraced my life and I started loving it!

When I returned home from the beach, my final divorce decree was in the mail. On August 19, 1997, David and I were divorced.

For me, this was the beginning, a chance to start fresh but stronger and wiser. My reality was clear. I was not going to be a married woman with children! So I absorbed myself in the things I knew would bring me joy and fulfillment.

My days started with a prayer of thanksgiving to God for a restful and peaceful night and another beautiful day. Then after a look at myself in the mirror, saying with a smile, "I love you," and excited to start the day, acknowledging and loving myself, I felt empowered!

Then out of the bed to start my morning regime now that my mental and emotional barometer were on "excellent," I was ready to spruce up the exterior with a long, hot shower, spending several minutes enjoying the water running over my body and washing the little bit of hair I have. It is very uncommon for black women to wash their hair every day, but I do and I love it. I need it, I feel fortified by the cleansing from the top of my head to the bottom of my feet. It is exhilarating and I don't think I could live without it. For close to twenty years of strange looks, whispers, and compliments, I felt confident that I must wear my hair short. It is the only way for me, no matter what anybody else says. I accepted my reality of being a woman with very short hair and if I met a man who wanted a woman with hair longer than a fade from the barber shop, he didn't want me. I was finally secure in not fitting the mold of public opinion.

Then into the closet to select my attire and that was not always easy, but always fun. I had adorned myself with a fine wardrobe that fit my taste and my wallet. Dressed and feeling great I was out the door, into my clean and shiny Beamer, and off to work. My first stop was court, for another day of trials relating to the custody, support, and visitation of children. Then into the office to talk with new clients who poured out their hearts to me as they described, in great detail, the pain and disappointment of losing a love they thought would last forever.

If I hadn't felt good when I left home, after a few hours of hearing and absorbing the pain of others, I would have quickly drowned. I had to be grounded in my reality because other people were depending on me to help them navigate their love challenges while fighting over the children, the cars, the house, and the possessions. I realized that all of the fighting was just a symptom of trying to mend a broken heart, of trying to capture some of the love that once existed. The cars, the children, and the possessions are unfortunately just the pawns in the game of trying to survive the pain.

I was now thirty-seven and well on my way to self-satisfaction, recalling the events of the past, building on them, and vowing never to make those same mistakes again. I was living with love without being in love with a man.

I had fought to have contentment and I finally had it. I knew it was because I had the natural desire to survive and I overcame my pain and disappointment by implementing a lifestyle. This lifestyle included doing things that empowered and motivated me, like writing in my journal, dining out at fine restaurants, going to church, practicing family law, watching the sunrise, dancing and singing. My survival tactics were working and I continually used them.

I encourage everyone to celebrate their life because no one is a mistake, and everyone plays a vital role in the book of life. Success is not measured by our education, income, or size of our home. I have measured my success by the positive impact that I have on people's lives. The best gift in life is the love of sharing with self and others!

The survival tool which I consider to be my strongest tool is nature. After Daddy died, the sky became my source of strength. I can always look up and find power. I look at the clouds and I feel peace and tranquility; when I look at the sun I find the strength to persevere and the courage to overcome; when I look at the sky, I sense the power of God watching over me; when I look at the stars, I feel joyful and a sense of freedom, an urge to dream and soar; when I look at the moon, I feel courageous; when I look at the ocean I have visions, and my dreams become reality in my mind; when I look at the mountains I know I can endure. I have treated nature as my source for survival because it endures all seasons.

After losing the physical love of a man, I was forced to learn how to live by loving something that will never leave me. I discovered that I could feel joy and contentment with things other than a man. I learned to love and really appreciate nature. I enjoy looking at the sky and feel happiness and peace as I admire how God paints the clouds across the sky differently each day. I feel secure when I look at the sky at night and see the beautiful stars and planets lit up like diamonds. They provide me with a visual presence reflective of my inner strengths: the ability to overcome and conquer, the ability to have peace, joy, contentment, and happiness, without the necessity of being married. I had my faith in God that He would keep His promise and never leave me. I was in love!

Without my survival tactics and my desire to conquer my obstacles in life, I most certainly would have been a bitter, angry woman with low self-esteem. I know because I have seen the casualties of a broken heart.

Trying to survive a divorce in a society that thrives on marriage and family can be so very difficult for many people.

My survival tactics kept me stable and allowed me to slowly accept that I was not fitting into the crowd. I was not married with children. I was divorced, not once, not twice, but three times.

Being divorced and accepting that reality was a daily task. I had to learn that if I wanted to enjoy life, I had to accept that I could have a fulfilling and thriving life without being part of a couple.

Being a member of a church has always been a part of my life. I have literally been in church all my life — one lady, Pat Drayton, often reminds me that she held me on her lap in church when I was just a baby. And I am still in church. Church has always been a place I have enjoyed. I have sung in the choir, ushered, attended numerous Bible classes, served on numerous committees, taught Bible class, and taught new members. No matter what happens in life I intend always to be a member of a church. The church provided me with the foundation I needed to grow spiritually and emotionally.

Church allows me to sit down and listen to the voice of God through the words of my pastor, Bishop Walter S. Thomas, Sr. Church is where I can sing, shout, pray, and rejoice about my life, reflect on my trials, face my fears, and seek hope to fulfill my dreams.

However, I confess that church has also been one of the hardest places for me to feel comfortable about being divorced.

Church is a place that is generally filled with an ideology that marriage is the only true way of life. I will not, however, debate the ideology of the church. I will say that I believe there are more people than most would like to think or admit who are married, go to church regularly, and are unfilled in their marriages. Some cheat, and many only dream of finding true love with their mate. Sad, but true.

I chose not to hide behind the title of married and unhappy. I stood up against the stigma of divorce. I had to be courageous in accepting that I was different; otherwise, I could be a casualty of my broken heart, left with feelings of low self-esteem and failure. It was not easy or pleasant. Sometimes church people can be the worst critics and the loudest skeptics. I have a friend at church who started calling me "Liz" years ago, after my second divorce. She called me Liz after Elizabeth Taylor, who is probably the most famous divorcée. I was never upset by the nickname because I knew Elizabeth Taylor knew something about love, because nobody would get married eight times without being in love with love. I was like Elizabeth Taylor and I embraced the nickname. Although she was divorced multiple times, she experienced love and the pain of losing, and she valiantly survived. Even after eight divorces, Elizabeth Taylor said, "I hope to fall in love just one more time!"

Accepting reality and adjusting to it takes courage, time, and perseverance. I had to be courageous in the face of people talking about me. I learned that a man who inquired about me was told that I was "the woman of many last names." I was hurt when I learned of this description, but I overlooked it because the reality was I had three different married names, and the reality was I couldn't change that fact. So I accepted the reality and dismissed the comment because even with my "many last names" I knew I was loved, and I do not regret the experiences which had given them to me.

Many people do not understand that a divorce can often be like the death of a loved one. There is a period where you grieve and suffer the emptiness of the relationship being gone forever.

The deaths in my life also taught me how to accept reality. After Daddy's death I learned that there was nothing I could do to change the reality of his death. I had to live with it or die because of it. My grief was a transition and living through the natural sequence of events taught me to be strong, no matter what happens and no matter who is with me or not with me. I accepted that I grieve hard and I am a crybaby because I hate it when the people I love die. However, I accept that as a part of life that I must cope with.

My grief led me to revelation about myself which was something I needed. I learned that in life I must be strong enough to endure, too scared to fail, and smart enough to accept reality.

I embraced my reality and I am grateful that I survived. Clearly my early survival tactics had become a way of life for me, enabling me to have a solid foundation for survival and a springboard for my wholeness.

After many years of sleepless nights and tears, I had accepted the reality of my life. I knew I had no other choice but to embrace my three marriages and divorces or drown in regret.

♥ ♥ ♥

Since my divorce, Phillip and I had been spending more time together. We dined out frequently, and shopped in exquisite stores together. We attended the same church and enjoyed worshiping God together. It was a lot of fun. After sixteen years, I was finally introduced to his family. Phillip had proven himself to be a true friend to me.

Now with my reality clear, I was ready, yet again, to tackle my desire to love. What was I going to do with the love in my heart? Should I get married again?

Chapter 6

"Fragile, Handle with Care"

I was only thirty-eight and, although divorced three times, I couldn't call it quits on love, could I? I still wanted to be in love, in a healthy, satisfying relationship. I was now fully equipped, knowing what I did want and knowing what I did not want.

I knew that I did not want a man whom I could not trust. The only way for me to know I can trust someone was over time and through experiences together. It's a funny thing — you never know how a person will act or react until an event presents itself. I knew that people could disguise their identity and it could take a lifetime to really get to know someone. Nonetheless, even if it took forever, I was determined to be only with a man I could trust.

I would not want to be in a relationship with someone who was selfish, immature, without a sense of humor, and permanently broke.

I knew what I wanted and I didn't have to be married if it meant settling for a dysfunctional relationship in the name of marriage.

I spent my time enjoying my life, a demanding job, active church involvement, writing a book, and seeing Phillip. I was busy and though everything appeared to be fine, there still was some unfinished "love business."

I knew that I had a fantasy of Phillip and me one day getting together. But I never gave any thought to our getting married because he never made our relationship a priority. Now things were different. We were seeing each other every day. We had dinner regularly at his mother's house.

I was still not clear about whether I should get married again. I believe God's directives about marriage as stated in the Bible, that "the two will become one . . . therefore what God has joined together, let no one separate" (Matthew 19:5-6). I believe now and I have always believed that marriages which survive time do not equate to a marriage made by God. Many people are very unhappy in their marriage but, because of religious beliefs and the scrutiny of others, they will not divorce. I also have been blessed to see and recognize many marriages which I know are created by God. These marriages have a sincerity within them which exudes their true love, versus the outward appearance that people portray in public, which can be seen by a wise eye as only a show to an outside world. I do not advocate divorce. I would have liked never to have been divorced. However, I made a choice to live my life with the scar of divorce and to find peace and contentment with the scar.

For many years my question was whether marriage was required for me to be within the will of God for my life. I wanted to be married but was that what God wanted for me?

The reality of marriage and divorce had consumed my life for eighteen years. It had become a way of life for me, marriage then divorce, marriage then divorce, marriage then divorce. If I was clear about one thing, it was that I never wanted to experience divorce again. I struggled to find peace with my faith, knowing and believing that divorce was not condoned in any religion. It was hard watching my clients labor through the process of learning to accept the reality of a dream come true of love and happiness that turned into an unimaginable nightmare of heartache and disappointment.

In divorces, the names of the parties are different; however, the circumstances of and reasons for the problems are always the same: a failure and refusal to meet the expectations of a spouse, and selfish and dishonest motives.

Love, marriage, and divorce were now my life's work, and I was getting a good view of the entire picture. It caused me to become very cautious about forming my own expectations for my love life.

I was seeing over and over again how couples operate. Whether married, or not married but with children, it was all the same — people dealing with their expectations for love and then disappointment. I was coming to a realization about why some marriages end in divorce, why some marriages last with discontentment and deception, and why some marriages thrive with couples embracing and cultivating their love! To me it was clear that it all started with expectations and the willingness, unwillingness, or inability to fulfill those expectations.

The main reason Adam and I started to have problems was that I had the expectation he would be a faithful husband. He was having an affair and I was unwilling to accept it. On the other hand, there are some who know and accept that their spouse is having an affair. Some just wait, hoping and praying that it will soon be over; on some occasions, it does end. But I had a different expectation. I wanted Adam to end his affair, and he was unwilling to adjust his behavior and I was unwilling to adjust my expectation, so ultimately our marriage began to crumble. I could have remained married to Adam; I considered it. But my expectation of our marriage did not include him being incarcerated for life because of an act which he intentionally committed without considering the consequences.

I forgave him. I did not stop loving him, but I decided, without consulting God, that I did not want to live my life going back and forth to prison. I made the choice to believe that God's love for me would overrule my desire to divorce so that I could live with peace.

My expectation for my marriage with Solomon did not include a husband who would gamble his money away and become aggressive and violent when drinking too much alcohol. I accepted that Solomon had limitations. I made a choice to divorce him, knowing God had warned me not to marry him.

Solomon and I were divorced because I would not adjust to his sporadic fits of anger and I expected to live free from verbal and physical abuse.

David and I were divorced because I refused to adjust to his life as a new father, created by his adulterous relationship. I could have adjusted, but I chose not to! I accepted that I was a person who would not adjust to living with betrayal, drama, and doubt. I realized that once trust is broken in a relationship it is never solid again. Trust is a necessary and valuable asset for a successful and rewarding relationship.

Adjusting and compromising are choices and, depending on the circumstance, they can be easy or impossible.

I hope that no one perceives me as unsympathetic or intolerant when I describe my reasons for divorcing, because every one of us has limitations. My limitations include an inability to accept dishonesty and betrayal. I know how to forgive and I also learned how to protect myself. Sometimes life requires hard choices.

I made a choice to have happiness while living versus living unhappily married. I was not going to be happy trying to cope with David and Melanie raising their son. It was my expectation that David would not have any more children. It was my expectation that David would be trustworthy and faithful to me. Maybe if David had been my first husband,

I could have accepted the mistake and gone forward with our marriage despite his infidelity. But I had already experienced the pain of betrayal with Adam and I feared self-destruction. It was very difficult to consider divorcing David. It was my third marriage and who, except maybe movie stars, gets divorced three times? I shuddered at the very idea but I found myself evaluating my limitations, considering my expectations, charting my goals, and, for the first time, seeking God, and I divorced David.

Regardless of the reason for the divorce, the etiology of the divorce can be found in the unfulfilled expectations of one or both of the parties. They realize they cannot live or no longer want to live with the present and unforeseen circumstances which only bring them pain.

I would often counsel my clients on how the reality of marriage is slow to become clear. At the altar, at a ceremony with friends and family, everyone is caught up in the excitement of the moment, but the reality of the commitment does not reveal itself until much later!

In the first days and years of marriage, all couples are required to make some adjustments. It is never a question of whether adjustments should be made; it is the reality of the commitment that requires adjustments to be made! Adjustments in thinking, behavior, character, and routine are required; slowly it becomes clear that married people live very differently from single people.

It is a fact that if couples do not make adjustments that accommodate each other's needs and expectations, the marriage will ultimately transform into a den of madness. People must learn how to be good spouses. If people refuse to adjust to the expectations of their spouse, trouble will follow.

Every day I was listening to people talk about their marriages, their baby's daddy, their baby's momma, all professing some level of hurt, fear, or anger. They were people who, for the most part, had good intentions, but along the way their intentions dissipated into pain and drama!

I was scared about even considering getting married again. I knew I didn't want to be divorced again, so how would I avoid it?

♥ ♥ ♥

By 1999 Phillip and I had been dating two consecutive years. It was a satisfying relationship. We socialized with friends, nurtured our spiritual relationship with God together, we laughed, we talked, we visited with his family, and, without saying it, we loved each other.

Yet, for the very first time in my adult life, I was not waiting for the relationship to move into marriage. I was satisfied with myself and was not looking for love with a man to make my life complete and fulfilling. I was already complete, filled with my sincere and natural love for self and others. Equipped with my survival tools, I had everything I desired in life: family, good health, spiritual grounding, a rewarding career, and lots of great friends. I had everything I needed, including love. For once I realized that it was not necessary for me to be married to be satisfied and content with my life.

Finally, I was in love with me! It took years and it took hard work, confronting my deepest fears and my most dreaded pain, but it happened.

I was now thanking Adam, Solomon, and David because I was finally loving myself. It was through our marriages and divorces that I learned to love myself completely and unconditionally. I accepted my role in my marriages and my divorces. I refused to blame them and I refused to blame myself. I accepted that we both made some mistakes, but our intentions were always to love each other. I was grateful to them for being a part of my journey.

On August 17, 1999, I was thirty-nine, just one year before the big four-zero and I was so excited. When I was growing up my mother had said to me on many occasions, "Life begins at forty," and I was expecting for just that to happen. I was already well on my way!

I vowed to enjoy the last year of my thirties enjoying being me!

Phillip bought me a telescope for my birthday, and I was thrilled. He knew that I was fascinated with looking at the moon and stars. I considered it very thoughtful.

Life was so very good. I was enjoying every aspect of my life; then, in October 1999, one of my best girlfriends, Cheryl, died from breast cancer. I was really shaken by her death. She was a beautiful young lady who had so much love in her heart, yet she never received the love she so richly deserved. She had also been married more than once. Her first marriage ended because of her husband's infidelity; however, she didn't recover like me. Instead his infidelity ate away at her confidence to the point where she had low self-esteem. She was married a second time but was still dealing with feelings of insecurity and a lack of trust in her mate. I was a stronger woman now but I was still distraught in so many ways. Why was it that she was never able to overcome or heal from her broken heart and overcome the betrayal in her marriage? I knew why; we had discussed it so many times: she had no self-confidence. She always thought there was something wrong with herself. No matter how many times I told her, I could never convince her that she was beautiful, valuable, and smart. I was hurt and grieving her loss. I felt that I had failed in helping her to overcome her low self-esteem. I began another internal quest to understand why some people die from their disappointments and heartbreaks.

I started to feel alone. Phillip was never a very emotional person. In the past, when I was grieving and needed to be cuddled, I had a husband to comfort me. This time it was different. I didn't have a husband and I was uncomfortable because I wanted to be comforted with hugs and kisses. However, that was not Phillip's personality. He was a comforter who offered some kind words of encouragement. I recognized that I desired more and I needed more.

As I talked with Phillip about my grief, I learned he had a cold opinion about death. He would dismiss the significance to a mere few words: "Well, they are dead now." I was shocked to discover his callous attitude. Clearly, we held very different expectations for how to cope with the death of loved ones. I rationalized that because he had been in Vietnam, this was his coping mechanism.

This was Phillip's first up-close and personal interaction with me and grief. I wanted him to adjust and cope with my grieving by consoling me with long strong hugs, but he didn't, so I accepted it. I continued loving him, and worked through my grief without him, wondering if I could live with this behavior throughout my life.

I have a very large family. I still have three great uncles and four great aunts living, two uncles, eight aunts, over twenty first cousins and over fifty second, third, and fourth cousins. Death and funerals would be a big part of my life, and I expected my man to console me the way I desire to be consoled. What did this mean for Phillip and me?

On Thanksgiving 1999, Phillip and I attended church service and then had dinner with his family. I had established a strong and loving relationship with Phillip's family: his mother, father, aunts, uncles, cousin, daughter, her mother, and her family.

It was a great day, and I thought it was going well until I was listening to the Temptations. They were singing about love and one stanza in the song said, "I would die for you." Phillip replied in response, "I'm not dying for anybody." Wow, it was an unsolicited blunder that I never expected. It was a beautiful song. Why did Phillip say he wouldn't die for anybody? Was he talking about me? Did he mean he wouldn't die for his wife? Maybe it meant nothing. . . .

Early in the morning on November 28, as usual Phillip called me. We started our conversation in our normal fashion with "Good morning, how are you?" Then, without any warning, Phillip said, "I'm ready to get married, are you?"

Bam! I was not expecting Phillip to say anything about marriage. I guess it was a proposal but I was shocked! During the last two years Phillip and I had never talked about us getting married. It was a subject he avoided. Although he had given me two rings, he made it very clear, on both occasions, that it was not an engagement ring.

Now, out of the clear blue, he was ready to get married. No proposal on his knees, no cute black ring box waiting for me to open, just the proposal over the telephone.

To say the least, I was stunned, but probably not as stunned as Phillip when I gave him my response.

"I need some time, maybe about two years."

It was the last thing I expected to say to Phillip because I was certainly in love with him. I had admired him and loved him for over eighteen years. Phillip had allowed me to come into his heart and occupy a space that could never be filled by anyone except me, but I was not ready to marry him. Why?

I told Phillip I needed some time. I needed more time to define my expectations for myself, for him, and for us. I was certainly not going to get married again without knowing exactly what I should expect for my future.

For the past two years I had wondered whether I would ever get married again and, if yes, why.

I had married Adam, Solomon, and David for love, yet we still divorced. Why and what would make me marry again?

I was not sure what Phillip expected of me. He had never been married, had never really been in a monogamous relationship. Now he was ready to be my husband?

I was not sure what my expectations were for him. I had not given enough thought to him being my husband. I was enjoying our relationship just the way it was, with the expectation that it would continue to be fulfilling for both of us. Marriage could turn things topsy-turvy for us.

Should I have said, "Yes, I will marry you," and then we could discuss our expectations later?

Phillip told me, "I can't wait!" *Bam bam!*

Although shocked, I accepted Phillip's declaration without asking him why he couldn't wait.

I didn't think it was the end of our relationship. We had had an eighteen-year friendship and I did not expect this to be the end.

Our routine changed. Instead of seeing each other every day, we were seeing each other every two days. I took the time to identify my expectations for myself and my expectations for a relationship. Finally, I knew I had control, control of my emotions, my desires, and my doubts.

On August 17, 2000, I spent my fortieth birthday at the beach alone watching the sunrise. I had an epiphany: I am an independent woman, very strong willed, ambitious, enthusiastic, and a free spirit. I don't have to be married to be satisfied and excited about my life. I can be devoted. I can love forever, I know how to compromise, I love to laugh, sing, and dance, and I can have a fulfilling life with fulfilling relationships without being married. I can have everything I desire in life and if marriage is not a part of the equation than that's all right! I can live alone and love it!

It was not the fortieth birthday that I had expected twenty years earlier, but it was the fortieth birthday that I loved. I knew my life was in order and after three divorces I knew that I didn't need a husband to be a satisfied, joyful, successful lady.

I spent New Year's Eve with friends and I anticipated with excitement how my life would be at forty.

My law practice had grown tremendously and I was at a crossroads. I had to make a decision to hire more staff or get out. I considered getting out of the family law practice because I was starting to burn out. Every day was a problem. Clients called day and night. I noticed I had started having a drink on Friday evenings and I was now using profanity. I loved my clients but I was stressed out coping with their lives.

I closed my family law practice and joined the law offices of Saul E. Kerpelman & Associates, P.A. For the past four years our offices were next door to each other. I had had many conversations with some of the staff and attorneys as we passed in the hall and gathered at the elevator. It was perfect. The firm represented people who had injuries from childhood lead poisoning. It was something new and I was thrilled.

In December of 2001, I purchased my first house. I was forty-one years old and the only reason I had never purchased a house earlier was that I always expected to buy a house with a husband. For years I had lived in apartments because I could not see myself buying a house without a husband. It was my self-created self-limitation that was without merit!

Phillip and I were still talking on the phone and we saw each other in church. I knew that we would never rekindle our love in the same way.

I began to fill my house with me. I had only one requirement for my house, and that was a wood-burning fireplace. And I got it. On the night I settled, December 21, 2001, I went to my empty new home, made a fire, and slept on the floor. I was all alone and I was content!

The new millennium was a fresh start with new revelations. I was divorced and single for five consecutive years, dating but not seeking marriage.

I understood that I possessed a deep love for others and myself. I could love freely and consistently and I did not have to be married. I did not have to have children to experience the essence of love. I now had two nieces, three godchildren, and a host of other people's children whom I loved like my own. I still had my friends, both male and female, who had traveled with me through the good and the bad. I was still experiencing love and loving, and I was content doing it and not being married.

In 2002 Phillip and I stopped seeing each other, although we remained friends and have periodic conversations. He continued to call and check on me and we continued to see each other in church.

It seems that my mother was correct. Life did begin at forty. As the years passed, life continued to be blissful. I dated and did not fall in love with a man. I kept loving myself and enjoying my life. I did some traveling. I spent time entertaining my friends. I danced, I sang, I laughed, I embraced my life.

In March 2008, Adam celebrated his fiftieth birthday. I visited him in jail. It was a special occasion for him and I knew that he would be pleased to see me. It was surreal, looking at him and knowing that he had spent over twenty-five years in jail. His skin was still smooth and clear, as if he had never had a day of trouble. His hair was now grey, as he was prematurely grey like his mother, although life in jail probably accounted for some of it also. He was still good looking and I still loved his smile. Throughout the years Adam and I enjoyed our visits with each other; we were always happy to be together. Although I do not visit often and we do not write consistently, except maybe a birthday card, and we do not talk on the phone, we have continued to share a close relationship and our love connection still exists. I still have a close relationship with Adam's mother and his two brothers. We shall forever be family.

I joined Solomon and his family in the celebration of his father's seventieth birthday. I love his family, his mother, his father, his three brothers, and his aunt. We too share a bond that can never be broken.

David and I have remained close. I hired him on several occasions to make repairs and upgrades to my home. On one visit, David brought his son, Emanuel. This was my first time seeing Emanuel since his birth. He was eleven years old.

One time Monica saw Emanuel with his mother and David. From that point on she always said to me, "That is not David's son. He doesn't look anything like him." I would laugh and I told her, "Yes, it is his son." David never had a paternity test. Melanie was married at the time. Who knows? It didn't matter to me.

I welcomed Emanuel into my home. I would never mistreat him. He knows only that I am his father's ex-wife. David has been active in Emanuel's life and I was proud of him. David had stopped seeing Melanie when Emanuel was still a baby, but he had been committed to being an active father. I told David that he could bring him by any time. He was a handsome young man and I loved children. I developed a loving relationship with Emanuel. It is strange how life can be, because I never expected it. I truly love the young man. We share a special bond: I call him my dance partner and whenever he comes to my house I turn on some music and we dance together. I see how David devoted more time to being a father to this young man than with his other children. My prayer was answered because Emanuel loves David and considers him a good father. I have had no contact with Melanie, although she knows that Emanuel has a relationship with me.

I am convinced that I will never totally disconnect from Adam, Solomon, or David. I still love each of them and I know they still love me.

At fifty-one years old I was still single. I do not make commitments easily but I have healthy, mutually rewarding relationships. I am still not ready for marriage again, not yet.

I have taken control of my emotions. I live in harmony with myself,

God, family, friends, and peers, every day. I do not allow people to create pain and havoc in my life. I do not live in an environment that is unpleasant or without peace and joy.

After discovering what love means to me, I discovered my limitations, and one of my limitations is falling quickly and deeply in love.

I now understand that I am fragile! I do not expect others to handle me with care. It is my responsibility to handle myself with care. My bosom contains some grief from the loss of loved ones and some heartbreak from disappointment, but it is all buried deep down in my soul, only to remind me that I am fragile. I am ever so mindful, and yet not angry. Pain can fuel anger, anger can fuel hate, and hate can fuel destruction. I learned to handle my pain delicately so that I would not be angry. I learned to handle my pain purposefully so that I could understand and accept the reality that love can hurt. And, I learned to handle my pain meaningfully, so that I could grow and learn from the experience.

Chapter 7

Finding Serenity

It was a long and sometimes tough road, but I made it. I found serenity. I am fifty-three years old, single, and really having the best time of my life.

Serenity is not a house, a career, a spouse, children, income, or notoriety, although these things can certainly add to our life and bring us joy. However, things and possessions do not equate to serenity. Serenity is what can never be taken away from me.

Serenity is having peace and joy on the road I travel. Every morning when I wake up, I am happy! I smile every day and, if I am not smiling, it is because I am bearing the weight of hurt: someone I love is sick, in trouble, or has died.

I possess serenity because I love my life and the people in it. I have serenity because I have no regrets about my life. If I could, the only thing I would change in my life is that the people I love would never die.

I have found serenity in growing older. Living through my forties was fun, rewarding, and exhilarating! I didn't get married, although Phillip did and so did David. I am happy for them both. I know that it is good to have an ending because it allows for a new beginning. I am also very glad that I do not have to ponder if we will be together because those chapters of my life are closed. The only thing that remains is a friendship that is full of love that will be treasured forever.

I have serenity because I learned to adapt to circumstances and situations with a positive outlook. I learned how to manage my thoughts because negative thoughts can paralyze and cripple growth. If I had allowed myself to focus on the negative things that people would say about me, I would not be where I am today.

If you allow your mind to focus on the wrong things you will walk the wrong way. My thoughts are always filled with good things, thoughts of success, of helping others, about being grateful. It is easy for me to think positively. I use my survival tactics, which are simple yet powerful for me: listening to the birds singing, feeling the softness of the morning wind and the calmness of the night air.

If you clutter your life with violence, drugs, depression, despair, confusion, negative people, and physical and mental abuse, you will hear the loud voice of defeat, and you will never secure your destiny in life.

I have serenity because I live without the notion that I must please other people. My mother desired for me to have been married only once. I would have loved to make her proud in that way, but I decided I had to live my life to please myself and not her. I refused to be controlled by the public opinion about divorce and the labels that are often attached. I have serenity because God has still given me health, strength, a sound mind, love, joy, peace, a little money, and lots of laughter, even though I have been divorced three times.

I have serenity because I love the lady that I have become and the strong characteristics that I have developed. I respect people and I accept the choices they make for their life. I accept the limitations that others possess and I do not expect more than what people are capable of giving.

I found serenity in knowing that I am loved and I know how to love.

I found serenity because I have no regrets. Over twenty years ago I made a choice not to have children and I am glad because when I was in my twenties and thirties I was struggling to find clarity in my life. At the time, I was unprepared to be a good mother. I have never regretted the decision. Today I have more children than I ever imagined.

I have serenity because I am true to myself by following my dreams and working to achieve my goals. Earlier this year I broke off my relationship of four years. It is not that anything was wrong, but I knew I had a road before me that I wanted to travel alone.

I have serenity because I do not want to be anybody else, except myself. There can only be one Oprah Winfrey, only one Anderson King, only one Barack Obama, only one Angelina Jolie, only one Hillary Clinton, and the list goes on. I have serenity in knowing that I love myself just the way I am.

The key to finding serenity is discovering who you are. What makes you sad? What makes you laugh? What makes you cry? What scares you? What fascinates you? It can take years of deep, honest, and sometimes painful reflection but the reward is worth the journey. Look in the mirror each day and look at yourself and learn to love what you see, no matter what somebody else says. I believe everyone is beautiful when they have peace and joy, when they love themselves and others. Discover your own rhythm in life and let your melody be heard by all who encounter you!

I have serenity because I never allowed myself to think that I was a failure. No matter what other people thought or said, I have never thought of myself as having failed at marriage. My marriages ended in divorce but the love that created those marriages continues and I consider that success. So many people who are divorced have acrimonious relationships. Even people who have never been married, but have children together, have no love for one another. The reality is I never stop loving anyone.

I would like to get married again, one day. I would like to get married barefoot on the beach. I want to feel the sand under my feet. It may happen and it may not, only time will tell, but this one thing I do know: in the meantime I will constantly strive to love myself.

I am unwilling to settle for a marriage filled with confusion, dishonesty, infidelity, and selfishness.

I believe that in life there are many opportunities to love, but there are usually fewer opportunities to be loved. Life is fleeting and every moment is precious and I vow to love every day.

I do not profess to know everything about love, but what I do know is I love being in love! What is surprising to me is that I have now been divorced almost sixteen years and I never imagined I would be so happy single.

When the stars are shining brightly
My heart is filled with Joy
When the wind gently blows
My soul is filled with Peace
The intensity of love has captured my Spirit
I yearn to understand!
When everything seems right and nothing can go wrong
My mind chases the rainbow and never finds the end.
When all my doubts have disappeared
I surrender to the mighty power of love.

I have serenity because I know my heartaches and the experiences I went through to overcome equipped me with everything I need to love others freely and unconditionally.

I have no doubt that **TRUE LOVE NEVER DIES** because love is eternal and it has a rhythm that can never die!

The Rhythm of Love

When I think of you, I think of eternity.
My soul begins to sing the melodious rhythm
of our love and my heart yearns for more.
Our love has carried me deep
into the harmonious motion of time,
Where the only thing that matters is loving You!

Acknowledgments

It took me seventeen years to complete this book. During those years I received encouragement and support from many family members and friends. Too many to name, so if you said "that's good," "that's exciting," "let me know when it's coming out," I thank you! Your words gave me the incentive to persevere.

I especially want to thank Nancy Williamson, Flora Young, Sandy Adams, Denise Landrum, Elisa Ford, and Robert Taylor, Jr., for your assistance, time, and unwavering support for this book.

To my editor, Laurie Rosin, this book is now everything I desired and everything that God commanded because of your skills and talent as an editor. Thank you so very much!

To Ron Toelke of Toelke Associates, thank you for your elegant book cover and page designs.

To Sarah Novak, thank you for providing outstanding copyediting services; you and Ron put the icing on the cake.

To my pastor, Bishop Walter Scott Thomas, Sr., thank you for feeding me the word of God and supporting His will for my life.

To my mother, thank you for birthing me into a family full of love! You have been a good mother, I love you!

To my brother, thank you for ALWAYS being a supportive, loving, and protecting brother. You have never disappointed me!

To Denise Landrum, Mary Parnell Jones, La'Shon Brice, Sharon King-Dudley, Diann Cupid, and Kerry Brandt, thank you for writing "About the Author."

About the Author

Avalon Sequoia Brandt

. . . trusts the power of the Almighty to reveal the keys to life and to manifest power and determination. She reveres God and expresses love openly in all her relationships.

. . . is honest and transparent, tenacious and creative.

. . . has a fire in her to be great at all that she puts her hand to, from completing law school to starting her own law practice. Her passion and perseverance have taken her to the next level of her life.

. . . teaches that failed love affairs are part of the growth process. Something does not have to end well to be one of life's most valuable experiences.

. . . has lived through many challenges, obstacles, and disappointments without scars.

. . . is a lover of love and all that love entails. She remains open to love without the contradiction of reliving the past.

. . . has picked up the broken pieces of life and pursued new territory without compromising her belief — *Still I Love.*